First published 2015

ISBN 978-0-9935709-0-2

Printed and bound by Berforts of Hastings

A Hole in my Canoe

By Martin Hole, John Dinnis and Will Miller

Prologue
"After cricket"

By John

The two sensible Rustics and son George had decided not to follow our canoe. We carried on, though, towards the harbour mouth where the estuary of the Axe met the sea. The tide was ebbing strongly through the narrow opening and we were being whisked along rapidly. Martin should have been steering, but was fiddling with his life jacket. Even on some of our white-water rivers I don't recall travelling at such speed.

And then he was gone. He simply jumped over the side. The force of the water washed him sideways, but he had managed to grab the canoe rope as he ejected. The canoe snatched to a halt as he struggled up the loose shingle and out of the powerful current. I looked ahead where the disgorging estuary waters met a choppy sea. There was a standing wave that looked evil. I knew that he would now claim to have saved my life.

"Just as well the others didn't come after us, as I would have struggled to save their lives as well as yours," the predictable fellow uttered.

We lugged the canoe out of the sea and started to carry it the half mile back to where the others had responsibly decided to stop following our boat. We reflected on the course of events that had led to this adventure. It had all begun six years ago with the question "What shall we do after cricket?"

I had taken my family down to Sussex to spend an August weekend with the Holes at their farm. My children quickly joined up with Martin's twin daughters, Florence and Poppy, and their younger sister Romney. The twins, when we arrived, were trampolining on a dead sheep. Our triplets, Hattie, Issie and Rosie, had soon deposed the twins and started bouncing on the same woolly carcase. The combined weight of the excited little girls had caused the previously spherical sheep to deflate, the putrid gas escaping from the back end in coarse farts. While this might appear a little unsavoury, I believed that our children were fortunate to enjoy a feral upbringing, close to Mother Earth.

Julie and the three girls had arrived in our ancient bus, converted from a 54 seater into a traveller's home and sometimes used as evidence in the accusation that I am a bit of a repressed hippy. I had come down separately with son George, four ponies and my faithful dog, Ness. She is a black and white mongrel and is named after the beer, and not, as Martin will childishly quip, the pea. As the children had formed an independently functioning swarm and the wives were good friends, I was free to potter down to Pevensey Cricket Club. I found my host on their pitch, beneath the Roman walls of the castle, and watched the match in which he was playing. That was when I had asked the question.

"After cricket?" he replied, "We shall go to the pub as usual. What an odd question!"

"No, AFTER CRICKET," I carefully enunciated. He was looking a bit tired after his match, but frowned as he grasped the higher meaning. I was 50, and Martin four years my junior. Every year, since we were 19, we had toured the West Country with our old university college side, The Wye Rustics. Its cricketing pedigree stretched back to the 1930s. This lasting quality owed much to the loveliness of the locations and to the great fun and friendship of this form of the game. It was on Rustics that I first met him. During his first night with us he had managed to completely obliterate a chair while sitting down to an otherwise peaceful post-match supper. "Things" often happened when he was about.

Our days of competitive cricket were drawing to a close. Martin was, once, a fine cricketer, a MCC playing member and veteran of many league campaigns. Tall and broad shouldered, he had been a wild fast bowler, capable of bruising batsmen and then confusing them with profuse well-spoken apologies. On his first Rustics we had tried to teach him "to bowl at the stumps," using flip chart pictures of them with such written instructions as "aim here" appended. Our efforts went largely unheeded, as opposition batsmen were always red rags to this blue-eyed bull.

When batting, if he managed to connect, Martin struck the ball a massive distance. He tells a tale from a tour to play Uganda in 1994, in which he hit an enormous six off Lamumba, their ferocious fast bowler, during a match in Kampala. The ball had sailed out of the Lugogo Oval and into an acacia tree, where it struck and killed a roosting chicken. He paid the owner forty shillings and maintains that he must have made an over-generous offer, as the happy poulter offered to sell him all of the remaining fowl. In deference to Lamumba, it should be added that this was the only scoring shot Martin managed to play in what was a typically brief innings.

Pevensey's village cricket looked to be a good playing standard, but as I watched I noticed Martin's run up had become a truncated lope and his spell of bowling short and late in the day. Once athletic, he moved rigidly in the field. Worst of all, he batted with judicious care.

"No decent human bats above six," he was fond of telling anyone who would listen. His captain now put him at five in the order. This confirmed to him that he really was the shadow of his former self.

My own cricket career was fluctuating between an all-round role in the village first team and a more educational function, which might be less fun, in our second team. Martin had maintained my cricket improved with age, though he had not said this for several years. He had a heartening belief in the acuity of my brain, to which he had ascribed this success. I did not wish to rob him of this delusion. However, I too was beginning to suffer from sore knees and a stiffening of the lower-back, so would soon be missing out on competitive sports that I had always enjoyed. The question hung heavy between us as we repaired to the hostelry by the castle.

No further thought was given to the query once inside, as the beer jug circulated and the merry bar grew loud with male voices and relaxed laughter. Martin dispensed generous amounts of beer to the younger players in both teams, constantly issuing the cheerful instruction to "clear a space" if they were not consuming enough. We had missed supper by some margin and walked home, returning to the subject of our mutual physical deterioration. I maintained that the rate of his decline was much faster than the rate of my own. He agreed, citing his life as a sheep farmer as part of the reason. He then reminded me of our performance on the Exeter cricket ground earlier in the summer. "To save us from further humiliation," he asserted, "we really ought to find a new sport altogether." A slight bristling of his unkempt left eyebrow, a signal of impending fun, suggested he had one of his batty plans up his sleeve, but he said no more.

Chapter 1
The Cuckmere - Summer 2009

A mellow summer's morning saw the Dinnis and Hole families on horseback. With Julie, Gundrada, who is small, full of laughter and Martin's long suffering wife, took command of the seven children. They set out across the marshes that formed a nature reserve and made up the substantial part of Montague Farm.   Martin often described Gundrada as the reincarnation of Queen Boadicea. Julie and my own children merged seamlessly into the mounted Iceni troop. I watched from the hill and thought what fun they were having on what must surely be the most expensive form of transport ever to be found.

The fathers had some farming to do. We needed to "looker" the livestock from the vantage of the Honda quad bike. Martin was prone to long-winded enthusiasms, especially with regards to wildlife and natural history, and to elaborate plans, some of which could be wonderfully flawed. He began to explain his fail-safe policy on the prevention of "fly strike" in sheep, based on replacing chemical treatments with timely shearing, having, typically, just pointed out a large, gleaming emerald and blue emperor dragonfly, with the proclamation:

"Anax imperator! They can catch horse flies on the wing, you know. And they can make love in mid-air. Breathtaking!"

Strike occurs when blowflies lay their eggs in the fleece and emerging maggots burrow into the flesh of the sheep. It is a big problem for his beloved flock of Romney ewes, as the wetlands are managed for wildlife and so contain large fly populations. A recent exploration of Montague by the British Society of Dipterists had yielded more than a hundred and twenty fly species. This group of boffins had been discovered with their big nets placed over their own heads, protecting themselves from the legions of biting horse flies in one of the wet meadows.   Martin was delighted when shown a "pooter," a sort of aerated test tube into which a specimen could be sucked, containing one of these pestilent creatures which was extremely rare and had beautiful big soft green eyes. He is an unusual sort of shepherd.

He surveyed his flock with pride then, suddenly, his expression changed. Looking at a ewe that was frantically biting itself, Martin resembled Napoleon in the face of the Russian winter, the great strategist undone by Mother Nature. "Blow. That shouldn't be happening. We'll have to catch her," he said, or words to that effect, then muttered something about "holding on." He revved the engine and we shot forwards in pursuit of the fly-struck sheep at a ridiculous speed.

Quad bikes can be dangerous. There is a list of warnings on the mud guard advocating safe driving and the wearing of helmets. Carrying passengers is forbidden. The list also contained the warning not to drive under the influence of alcohol. On that particular morning, given the residual impact of the evening in the pub, we found ourselves breaking all the rules simultaneously. To cap this disobedience, I had been joined on the back of the quad bike by Flintoff, the sociable sheepdog, who spent the journey politely trying to push me from my seat. He then abandoned ship when the quad set off after the affected animal, leaving me to cling on for dear life.

Carrying a passenger makes steering rather difficult. Martin overcame this by using extreme acceleration during the short and terrifying chase, and then, having caught the ewe, by slinging its 80kg weight across the handlebars. He rightly claimed that mechanics was not his strongpoint and the steering did not improve through the addition of the sheep. However, it did, thankfully, make him drive much slower and, re-joined by Flintoff, we returned to the farm buildings where the sheep was shorn and given medication. It occurred to me that Flintoff was quite a wise dog in having nothing whatsoever to do with his Master's sheep chase. I, too, should have known that a "quiet trip round the stock" would involve some sort of hair-raising incident.

The Iceni had got back from their ride and we reunited for a delicious lunch prepared by Gundrada. The afternoon promised a rich adventure, as Martin had organised for us to take all the children in two canoes on a journey down a nearby river.

The river Cuckmere rises in the Sussex sandstone of the High Weald, near Heathfield, dropping quickly to the clay country below. As it nears the sea it cuts through the high escarpment of the sumptuous South Downs, one of England's most treasured landscapes and immortalised in Kipling's *Sussex* as;

"Our blunt, bow headed, whale-backed Downs...

Where the rolled scarp retires

And the Long Man of Wilmington

Looks naked toward the shires..."

We joined the river near the base of this extraordinary 226 foot tall chalk giant etched into the hillside, just north of the pretty "olde worlde" village of Alfriston. From our start point the Cuckmere's famous meanders wriggle through a conservationist's lexicon of designated protected areas, most recently trumped in becoming a National Park. A separate channel, dug in 1846, carries the river past the iconic ox-bow lakes and to the sea. An interesting debate was raging over the future course of the river. It was too expensive to maintain the flood banks of the 1846 channel, and a conservationist led movement wanted to see the river restored to its route down the old meanders, which were currently filling with silt. Removal of the flood banks would also allow the formation of salt marsh and a richer environment for wildlife than the current sheep grazed brooks. Martin had great sympathy with this move to restoring the valley to a naturally functioning river system. However, friends of his who farmed up-stream were against the idea, concerned about flooding and the consequent loss of productive pastures. He also had sympathy with them. The debate remained un-resolved, either in Martin's head or in the public domain.

Alfriston was to be our start and the sea our destination, using two fourteen foot long open canoes. I mentioned his understanding of mechanics earlier, and now must complain about his grasp of matters mathematical. He somehow intended to squeeze two large men and seven children, nine of us, into a space designed for a maximum of six people.

We had arrived too early for the turn of the tide in the river. While we waited, Martin, encouraged by the whoops of his daughters, suggested I had a go at a "seal entry." He explained that this was the manoeuvre by which a seasoned canoeist would launch his craft, sitting in the canoe and sliding down a muddy bank and onto the river. Having no experience of canoeing, I thought this sounded straight forward. The canoe was lined up and, before I had time to sit, it slid away with surprising speed. Having just about remained upright, like a Hawaiian surfer, for the slide, I pitched headfirst into the river as the boat hit the water. It sank below the surface, in defiance of an assurance that the double layered plastic skin should make the canoe "unsinkable." I added physics to the list of practical sciences not understood by my friend.

Meanwhile, my farmer's Argyll wellingtons, like the canoe, proved very good at holding water. I tried various swimming strokes, none of which were aided by the weighty wellies, and eventually made it ashore, having rescued the water-filled boat. My crew mates, still giggling pathetically, were of little help.

The tide was now up and we embarked on our journey in the two boats. Initially the river was narrow and intimate, but it grew as the spectacular chalk landscape broadened below Litlington, the last of the villages before we reached the sea. The children were excited, happily splashing each other as we descended easily on the current. Pulling alongside my canoe, Martin explained why the Cuckmere cut through the chalk of the Downs rather than the softer clay of the vale to the north, something to do with warm tropical seas, Africa colliding with Europe, ripples of up-thrust and a broken chalk mantle some 30 million years ago. Talk of plate tectonics and local geology were then curtailed by a small flock of oystercatchers, whose vigorous piping was a much appreciated natural interruption. Undaunted, he demanded the Latin name from the children. Florence teasingly mis-identified them as hoopoes and called out "Upupa epops," obviously having had to listen to her father's ramblings before.

"Haematopus ostralegus," he intoned monkishly, before revealing what you can learn about soil structure from looking at the beak of the oystercatcher. "Those that eat worms from the silt have longer beaks than those eating winkles from the abrasive sand."

"He is better at biology," I thought to myself, looking with greater interest at these black and white and red wading birds.

After an hour or so we came to the mouth of the river, which spilled over the cobbled beach between the towering white cliffs of the Seven Sisters. The dwindling summer sun on these exactly vertical pure white cliffs was exquisite. "The scenery here must be one of the natural wonders of the world."

"It is," said Martin before embarking on yet another tangent, his enthusiasm being irrepressible. "The formation of flint, which you can see bedded in thin lines through the chalk, has always had an air of mystery," he continued, to the assembled children. "We know it is formed from the silica left behind from the bodies of certain prehistoric sea sponges, but the famous Sussex fraudster, Charles Dawson, perpetrator of the faked Piltdown Man, offered a variation of this theory. He delivered a hollow flint to the Brighton and Hove Natural History and Philosophical society in1901, into which he had put a mummified frog. Later shrinkage of the frog suggested it wasn't mummified at all, but was in fact only recently dead. One explanation of the hoax is that a hole made in the flint by a prehistoric worm, called a piddock, may have allowed the later ingress of a tadpole which was, subsequently, unable to escape from the centre of the stone and so grew to adulthood trapped inside. I think it was much more likely that the body had simply been added later, to create the curiosity." Martin's ridiculous lecture stopped at this point as he noticed that out of a starting audience of eight, only one remained.

From the beach, Julie and Gundrada collected all the children to go home for tea and pony feeding. That left us to find our way back in the canoes to where the trailer had been parked, a mile back up the Cuckmere, in the nature reserve car park. I looked back up the river and observed that the high Spring tide was still boring down it out to sea. There was no way of paddling against such a flow. Martin had a mischievous look on his face.

"I think we will go this way," he said pointing to the static water of the cut-off meanders, or ox-bows, which wriggled across the valley back where we needed to go. We lugged the two boats to the top of the beach and down the other side, away from the sea, and prepared to launch. There were several signs littering the shore, always an indication of institutional nature reserves. One of them said "No Canoeing."

"Wardens won't be out at this time of day," said Martin confidently, as we pushed off the bank and into these deliciously calm backwaters. He then resumed his lecture on the "The Toad in a Hole" flint, now that I was his captive audience. "The presence of amphibians inside rocks had intrigued a geologist called Dr Buckland who, in 1825, had conducted a rather odd experiment, sealing 24 toads into cells of either hard or porous limestone for a year. Incredibly, some of the toads in the porous rock survived..." The lecture, so recently re-started, thankfully stopped again as our attention became focussed on a distant vehicle. We had only paddled a couple of hundred yards since launching into the meanders.

A white pick-up approached us from the direction of the reserve visitor centre. It had green insignia on its side. As it got closer to us we read "Seven Sisters Nature Reserve." The Warden got out of this vehicle and began to shout. We carefully steered to the opposite bank from him, safe that he would not wade across, and waved cheerfully while studiously pretending that we could not hear what he was saying. Martin pulled his hat low over his face before issuing an apology, keen not to be recognised. Points made, we continued on to where the Land Rover was parked. The Warden's remonstrations had added the thrill of subversion to our summer outing.

We loaded up the canoes and drove home to Montague, some twenty minutes away. This gave me the opportunity to phone Julie. She reported that Ness had gone missing, suspected of being on a Rabbit hunt. We had brought her with us because she had only just returned from a lengthy absence.

Back at Filston, our home and farm on the North Downs, she was used to wandering the Darent Valley freely. However, during the previous winter she had disappeared. After a month, and assuming her to be dead, the girls organised for a new dog to come to Filston, and so we acquired our bearded hairy-dog, Frindal. The day after she arrived, one of my neighbours called to say he had seen a black-and-white dog, looking rather emaciated, running along-side his tractor in a field next to an encampment of large caravans. We were thus reunited with a happy Ness. To prevent a repetition of what we assumed was a kidnap, we fitted her collar with a GPS tracker that could be monitored on our telephones. We would always know where she was, we thought.

A week or so after fitting the collar the alarm on the phone indicated that Ness was in Croydon, twenty miles away. I told Julie that I had phoned the Police and was heading off to collect her. Rather confusingly, Julie pointed at a black-and-white dog sleeping soundly in Ness's bed. The tracker was in Croydon, the dog was in Filston. The mystery was never resolved. We had since replaced the errant tracker, so Ness was quickly traced to the wood behind Martin's house as we returned to Montague in time for another Gundrada feast.

That evening we spoke of larger, wilder rivers. The problem of "After Cricket" seemed to have an answer.

Chapter 2
The Kentish Stour - January 2010

By Martin

Wrecking a canoe is a rite of passage in life. My first proper wreck was of a canvas and wood kayak in a rough sea off the coast at Seaford, near my home in Sussex, when I was fifteen. I had recently returned from a canoe course with the Royal Marines at Lympstone in Devon and fancied my chances, so my mother had dropped me at the seaside. I had surfed in on a rather large wave but was unprepared for the violent dumping that followed. The kayak was terminally splintered on impact with the pebble beach and I took a bit of a battering myself. I was surprised that my mother was not angry with me. She simply observed that it was "the sort of thing that boys need to do."

True, our adventures also have something of their origin in a post cricket match conversation on what sporting life we might embark on, once our cricketing demises were confirmed by our respective captains. A version of this theme took place in the pavilion of the Exeter county ground. It is also a story about John which illustrates his traits of cleverness, unflappability, determination and a particular appetite for trouble. John and I have both played for the Wye Rustics for over 30 years, and this long standing fixture was against the Devon Dumplings. They were once a collection of eclectic individuals like ourselves, but in recent years their team had been managed by a formidable and highly capable cricketer. Gone were the days of the affable "tea towel" Williams bowling loopers with Wingers Dingers behind the stumps. The match was now gruellingly competitive.

This game started at 11.30 on a very hot July morning. Our Captain, (whose name is Crazey, but who is anything but) having won the toss, had decided to bat first. After about half an hour of cricket in which we were dismantled by the grace and athleticism of two of Devon's finest Australian fast bowlers, John was sent out to bat with the score looking dire. There was over an hour of the morning session remaining. Crazey issued the pointless instruction to "try to stay in until lunch."

Unfortunately, this put a hitherto unlikely thought into John's head.

"I'll do my best, Skip," said John, and walked out to the middle, wind-milling his cricket bat at the end of his Neanderthal arm. His team mates knew that his batting could be pyrotechnic and watched with interest. Was he really going to whack these young Aussie fast bowlers out of the ground? Certainly the energy with which he swung the bat before facing his first ball indicated great intent.

An hour and a half later John was still out there, "blocking" stoically. "Keeping an end up" was too active a description. Hockey is John's main sport and his skills at that game gave his cricket an unorthodox yet often effective style. It was not pretty to watch, but it did enable him to be a doughty competitor. The opposition were in disarray. The Dumplings intensely capable captain, normally ruddy cheeked, had gone a sort of puce colour. A scandalous "faux-pas" had unfolded in the course of John's innings during the morning's play.

"In all my years of playing cricket I have never seen such an innings played," moaned the puce coloured man, as the teams broke for lunch. Neither had we.

The Rustics, not looking one another in the eye, clapped the Dumplings off the pitch for the lunch interval. Crazey was heard to mutter distractedly about whether the fixture would ever be renewed. John came off the pitch looking cool and pretty pleased with himself. Cool because he had not scored a single run in the whole hour and a half of his batting. Pleased, because he had definitely followed his skipper's instruction. While watching from the pavilion, many observations were made about his crab like batting performance, my favourite being that he looked like a spasming donkey plagued by a fly.

I sat with the donkey at lunch, though no one else would. I, alone amongst the two teams, was in awe of his absurd achievement. I was also aware that the situation had not made John very popular. In some men such a dismal show of obstinate determination would be confirmation of some terminal dreariness. However, something more was afoot on this occasion. John has a terrific appreciation of where the humour lies in almost any given situation as well as a delightful and scientific clarity of mind. I knew that this was the root of his extraordinary innings and not his admirable devotion to the skipper's instruction. A love of the absurd, which I admit I share with him, was here at play.

"John, what are we going to do when we no longer get asked to play cricket?" I asked, thinking about how likely it would be for him to play in this fixture ever again. We muttered about how no other sport could yield the humour and camaraderie of cricket, nor capture so gracefully the sumptuous nature of hot English summers. Could golf measure up, we asked, as we contemplated our ageing bodies, or tennis, perhaps?

"What about canoeing?" I asked.

"Never done that, but actually I do love mucking about in water," replied John. That was very true and a most unpleasant image came to mind of a naked, ape-like Dinnis, followed by a baboon-like troop of naked Rustics including myself, plunging into the trout lakes at St Marybourne in the Hampshire Downs. The pink ensemble had swum vigorously out to a post in the middle of the pond which carried a sign saying "Private Fishing, No Swimming." In fact, such was John's love of a dip that we thought him to be semi-aquatic, a sort of human seal.

"I had a canoe in my twenties," I told him, but before I could regale him with a story concerning the misreading of tide tables and the late arrival at a wedding where I was to have been an usher, covered in oily mud and wearing an ill fitting wet suit, it was time for him to go back out to bat in the after lunch session. Needless to say, he was out for nought. That brought me to the crease and I too scored nought, but efficiently, facing only one ball. Re-selection for the fixture looked unlikely for either of us.

Six months later, pre-dawn, our two farm land rovers arrived at Pegwell Bay, the wilderness at the mouth of the River Stour in East Kent. It was January, sub-zero and the countryside covered with snow was in the grip of a big freeze. I had one of the open canoes on the roof-rack and we were about to paddle from Wye, the village near Ashford where both of us had studied, via Canterbury and out across the East Kent marshes to the sea. This was our first January expedition, and our preparation had been thorough. By that I mean John had booked somewhere to stay in Canterbury and I had acquired a nearly water tight barrel in which to put Mars bars, a towel and a second pair of corduroy trousers.

We launched the boat from the Tickled Trout, the pub by the bridge in Wye village, having first had a look at the lovely old college where each of us, at different times, had spent a happy three years. It now stood derelict and un-cared for, although snow covered the worst of the disrepair, having recently closed as a result of a sad amalgam of University politics, agricultural recession and planning intrigue. Its closure had also had a significant impact on Rustic cricket. The tour was traditionally bolstered by the best students from the college, but it had been shut for nearly a decade and the team was now struggling to find young recruits. Our youth were increasingly being conscripted from the sons of Rustics and their friends. The dilapidated college formed a poignant moment to start the adventure.

The river Stour below Wye cuts a meandering course through the stunning setting of the North Downs, whose woods and billowy chalkiness cloak the valley with natural grace. It then wends its watery way through three of Kent's most beautiful estates, Olantigh, Godmersham and Chilham Castle, before it enters the city of Canterbury. Clear water and a gravel bottom provide good habitat for trout, for which this stretch is highly prized and protected. January is the closed season for fly fishermen, so we thought we could descend the river without controversy. I should add here that I am an optimist of wholesome hew and have a firm belief that all plans will work out in an orderly procession towards success. John is a wiser man. He smirked at my assertion that our trip should be trouble free.

We took the river through the parkland of the first of the three estates and then, slightly to our surprise, through the formal gardens that surrounded the lovely mansion. The snow lay hushed on the trees and over the ground, causing strange malformation of the statues that adorned the cultivated landscaping. The water provided a delicate ribbon of blue and grey-green colour in this fabulous vista of pure winter whites and diamond icicles. We were privy to a private treasure. Fortunately we passed unnoticed by the occupants. This was an exhilarating, bejewelled, winter scene of surreal brilliance.

With just the two of us in one canoe my plan for the trip had included a cunning scheme to avoid hearing one of John's many tales about his disappearing dog, Ness. John was inexplicably proud of the dog's disappearances, probably because it was an ability that he shared with the animal, and he would get crotchety with me if I ever suggested that the dog's name derived from a pea. My scheme, which would also mean we would converse on subjects other than farming, was that each of us would prepare a "special subject" to be delivered during the trip. John's subject embraced the lyrics of Joni Mitchell and my subject was world-wide winds. Words from the great songstress were now swapped with my descriptions of the Ghibli and the Harmatan, the Sundowner and the Freemantle Doctor.

Lost in bizarre conversation and appreciation of our frozen setting we were brought scarily back to reality by an explosive volley of gunfire. We were now headed into the second of the estates. The reasons for John's smirking became apparent. Fly fishermen don't hibernate in the winter, they go shooting instead. There would be a gamekeeper and at least 20 beaters ahead, scandal and confrontation beckoned.

My mind turned rapidly from Brubus and the Haboob, and John's from the tuneless lyrics he had been declaiming. He started to paddle vigorously before I had generated a plan of action. This caused the boat to turn sharply. The canoe slewed onto a submerged iron spike attached to a large sign saying "No Canoeing." We were directly in front of the grand house, at the foot of its great snow-covered lawns. We needed to get out of this place before we were found by anybody and, most importantly, avoid the gamekeeper and his entourage of guns.

The spike carved a wound in the plastic as we corrected our line, but only a superficial one compared to that which we feared might be imminent if we were caught. The guns had gone quiet, but then we heard the sound of an engine. The only estate road crossed a pretty bridge a hundred metres ahead, from which were afforded lovely views of the river, on which we bobbed like sitting ducks.

"Oh dear," I said to John, "I think the whole shoot is coming this way." We were paddling vigorously but increasingly into plain view, the only splash of colour against the snowy backdrop. We could not be in a more exposed position. The engine noise grew louder.

Praying for a miracle to save us from the approaching shooters, the opposite occurred. Rounding a meander, we put up from the water some hundred mallard and about four hundred teal. Mallard are noisy quackers and teal have a dry rasping whistle. The ornithologist in me gasped at the drama of this cloud of wildfowl before it dawned on us both that the birds circling over head quacking and whistling would certainly get the attention of the gamekeeper, even if he had not yet begun his pursuit of the trespassers in the canoe.

Our adrenalin surged and we comfortably out-paced the rate of the swift river flow. Two more bends and a minute or so of time and we were clear of the danger. Half an hour later we were ordering a beer at The Woolpack pub in Chilham. Whilst reliving the glittering beauty of the river in its winter garb and congratulating each other for the audacity with which we had avoided detection, we made the rather basic error of ordering a second beer.

After lunch, warmed, but feeling a little sleepy, we nudged the canoe down a drainage channel running from the inn back into the Stour. The plan here was that the trip to the pub enabled us to avoid a large mill weir, and so it came to pass that my advice to John to "be a little careful" on re-entering the main river went unheeded. He was humming a lyric both wordlessly and tunelessly. The drain entered the river just below the weir, merging with the swirling white water that had tumbled forcefully over the structure. This moving froth would pose no problem to an alert paddler, but, alas, neither of us fell into that category.

I was steering at the back of the boat but neglected to do anything when the first wave came over the side. I was laughing too heartily at John's sudden soaking. The second wave, finding us even more unprepared, managed to overturn the canoe.

As she overturned I saw the possibility of avoiding total immersion in the water and flung myself upwards into an over-hanging tree. I was left dangling with my feet in the water and watched as John, the boat and our dry barrel were washed briskly down the icy stream. Eventually he emerged, like Poseidon, from the freezing water. He had gathered all our belongings but looked panicky. John is almost supernaturally calm, so his face bore an expression I had never seen before. I put it down to an early sign of hypothermia.

"Hole, where are you?" He was looking down into the river and, of course, he could not see me. I was still dangling from the tree up stream, though the branch was beginning to bend under my weight. I was helpless with mirth. My laughter made him look up in time to enjoy the sight of his smug canoe buddy slipping from the precarious hold on the bending willow and into the arctic Stour.

We rescued the boat, tipped the water out, got back in and floated down stream to what looked like an abandoned factory, where we disembarked in order to change into some dry clothes. Assuming no one in their right mind would be out in these conditions, in a place like this, we both immodestly stripped off our freezing and sodden kit. Lilywhite and bare as God made us, standing in the snow, we then heard the voices of two men. They were uniformed men and were coming straight towards us. I had yet to extricate the dry gear from the barrel and was further delayed as we became engaged in conversation with the security staff of the now not-so-abandoned factory. Stark naked in the freezing cold, we stood politely hiding what was left of our modesty with our cupped hands. The ensuing communication was not easy but successful in so far as the police were not called. We were allowed to dress, and then the two guards rather huffily escorted us out of the premises. John and I hypothesised only briefly on how the security men might even now be describing this encounter. We later discovered that this little episode occurred in the village of Thannington Without.

We reached Canterbury without further ado, fully clad in reasonably dry clothing. The canoe had to be carried through the city centre in the midst of the winter evening rush hour. John chose to cross the road to our hotel between two buses, a crossing he made easily but which was life threatening for me, attached some fourteen feet behind. The bus driver was not experienced at avoiding canoes during rush hour in the snow. I made a mental note to not cross any more busy roads with John leading the boat.

The canoe was then safely stowed in the foyer of the old hotel. A hot bath and more warm clothes were in order. That evening we had arranged a supper with two good friends, Nigel, another member of the Wye Rustics, and Giles, a local farmer who was also an adventurer. He had joined Cam McCleay on his Ascend the Nile Expedition on the upper part of the river in Uganda. Cam's team, while travelling over 3300 miles, had succeeded in rafting down the colossal 140 foot drop of the Murchison Falls. Giles told harrowing stories of these spectacular rock-strewn rapids, where the mighty Nile squeezes explosively through a narrow gorge. He described a brutal river full of crocodiles, a crashing microlight aircraft and, tragically, a tale of murder. A group of rebel soldiers from the Lord's Resistance Army had ambushed a support vehicle and killed Steve Willis, a friend who was not even an expedition member. He had been helping with the rescue of a man who had broken his leg when the microlight, while ferrying supplies, had crashed into the rocks in the middle of the ferocious falls.

Throughout the evening John and I insisted that the Upper Stour and the rough water of the Chilham Mill were at least as scary as the Murchison Falls, and only our cleverness and cunning river craft had saved us from the dreaded gamekeeper. Giles is a shooting man and he conceded readily that we had indeed been through a near death experience on the second estate. A good dinner was had and we repaired to bed, in the shadow of Canterbury's glorious cathedral, tired and very happy.

My plan for the following morning soon required alteration. To avoid a long carry of the canoe through the icy streets, we had entered the Stour over railings and down a steep wall into the water beside the North Lane car park. The river was shallow but brisk enough for us to quickly discover the day's first obstacle; a low bridge with a shootable sluice. It appeared on our horizon at the same time as the sluice keeper from the Environment Agency, hitherto unseen, began to close the water gates. We, (I mean John), quickly calculated that the gates were closing at the right speed to crunch the boat in half if we carried on forwards, so we executed a nifty emergency halt. We forced our way back up the river against the freezing current and portaged through the snow-bound city. This all took a while. Several of the many pedestrians trudging along slushy pavements were intrigued, and amazed, when we said that we were off to Pegwell bay, over twenty miles away, in a canoe.

To the east of Canterbury is found a landscape left from the mining of coal. Large areas of mining subsidence have given rise to another of Kent's great wild treasures. Vast reed-fringed meres appear along the river, merging with even larger areas of fen and wet willow woods. In these snowy winter conditions the effect was fabulous. The river and adjacent lakes provided the only unfrozen areas for wildfowl and wading birds to feed in and the wetlands teamed with the querulous, gabbling fun of these great flocks. John had lived in Kent all his life and was exhilarated by this wilderness that he was discovering. Peregrines that may well have slept the night on the Cathedral spire were stooping on the ducks and a marsh harrier nearly flew into John's head as he relieved himself behind a tree. His initial annoyance at being "mobbed by an eagle" quickly gave way to boyish, awed enchantment.

A decent lunch at The Grove Ferry Inn preceded the misery of paddling the river across the bleakness of the East Kent Marshes. The river here had no prettiness and lost the winter drama of the earlier run. It sloughed its way through the flat lands of dull, snow-covered, dreary arable fields. A bitter wind blew fitfully, as it always does. Meander followed meander, marking the senescence of this lowland stretch. The paddle became hard work. Our conversation began to pick up on the rhythm of these monotonous bends. I returned to winds.

"The Tramontana is a cold wind from the north, getting its frigid charm from the Alps and the Apennines before blowing into the western Mediterranean."

John was not listening, nor was he playing by the rules. Switching from Joni Mitchell to Neil Diamond, he sang without melody, "I've looked at clouds from both sides now, from up and down, and still somehow, it's life's illusions I recall...." We negotiated another hair-pin bend.

"That's Neil Diamond," I told him. Apparently I was wrong, as Joni wrote and sang it first. Yet another meander wound its course.

"A Bora is a wind blowing into the Adriatic that can cause the sea to freeze." I said, emphasising the first syllable of Bora, slightly hoping to get one back on John. He appeared not to hear my dull tetchiness. Another corner came and went.

"I wish I had a river to skate away on," he retorted as we rounded yet another bend. I managed not to show any sign of appreciation of the wit. Yet another bend approached.

"Aaah, Pluck's Gutter at last," said John. "Aaah" is one of John's favourite expressions and used most often when he is excited or pleased about something. The utterance in its entirety was hardly up there with

"Livingstone, I presume", but it marked a triumphal moment. Pluck's Gutter is where the Little Stour meets the Great Stour and owes its name to a Dutch drainage engineer, Ploeg, who was buried nearby at West Stourmouth. We were making progress. The river widened and began to straighten.

The other occurrence to give us cheer was the apparent nearness of the Richborough cooling towers, as these marked Pegwell Bay and the finale of our journey. John had made a comment about the towers not seeming to be any closer than they were before. After a further hour of paddling, the towers remained unchanged in size. It was only late in the afternoon that we finally sat on the river beneath the mighty edifices, built in the '50s as part of the power station that burnt the Kentish coal. They reached more than a hundred metres above where we sat on the water, their enormity dwarfing us in our little boat. In the January twilight this was our last chance to see these amazing pieces of industrial architecture, as the towers were scheduled to be demolished. Lit by the low winter sun, against a backdrop of snow, the giant towers were truly impressive.

The light had seeped from the afternoon as we hurried to beat the tide to Pegwell Bay. We now faced another unexpected challenge. We could not complete the river loop through Sandwich, for it was too long a journey, nor could we cross the main road between Sandwich and Margate, a dual carriageway, in the diminishing light and in rush hour, especially carrying a dark green 14 foot long canoe. Many of the vehicles on the road were from the pharmaceutical factory at Sandwich where an aphrodisiac tablet, sometimes known as the "Pfizer Riser," was made. We had been warned not to inhale the fumes, the consequences of which would be highly embarrassing, so this was another reason to avoid the Sandwich loop.

Our only way to proceed was via a structure called the Great Sluice through which the Stour crossed under the main road. Beyond the sluice lay the upper salt marshes at the inland reach of the bay, where we wanted to go. Canoe and two large farmers bundled inelegantly over the eight foot high security fence. We then managed to get the boat down a concrete spiral staircase, through the enormous river-pipe under the road, and repeated the operation on the other side. In the book on "How to Canoe" there had been nothing about the skills required for getting the boat down and up spiral staircases.

The tidal channel on the other side of the sluice was a dramatically changed world. We found ourselves in rapidly moving sea water. It was getting dark in a way that was luminously alive, subtly coloured by a winter moon and the starlight bouncing off the snow of the salt marshes.

"This is it, total wilderness!" I said with excited spontaneity. The freezing January moonlight felt eerily pure. Powerful currents gripped our boat and ripped us out towards the wilds of the Bay. We were in a primal, intuitive-animal environment that was strangely dissonant with our modern lives.

"Look! seals!" we said to each other in unison. Suddenly surrounding the canoe were about 20 common seals, appearing and disappearing, their near human faces looking quizzically at John and me. Many feelings coursed through us from fear to an excitement bordering on ecstasy. This ranked, to my surprise, up there alongside my best-ever wilderness moments. I had seen elephants in the foothills of the Rwenzori Mountains of Uganda and golden eagles lit by storm sunshine in the extinct caldera on the Isle of Rhum. I believe that real wilderness has an elemental purity that is good for the human soul. Here we were, not just enjoying the sight of it, but the feel of being in the clutch of its processes. However, before I could get all philosophical on John, he remembered to produce the football that we had found by a school outside Canterbury, which he insisted the seals would juggle on their noses. He chucked it gently to the nearest seal, which treated it with the disdain it deserved.

The canoe was moving briskly on the racing ebb tide. The lights along the shoreline were now just distant twinkles. We were no longer paddling. Eulogising about wilderness is all very well, but survival must be pursued. I asked John if he thought we were "there" yet. A good mile off shore, sub-zero and dark was "there" enough for both of us, so we jumped out onto the mud flats. We then dragged the canoe over a mile back to the shore. After two long days of paddling, the mile hike through knee-deep wet mud in sub-zero temperature was exhausting. By sheer luck we came ashore close to where the Land Rover we had dropped off the previous day was parked. Exhaustion gave way to a comfortable elation once we were inside and the heating was up to maximum.

Chapter 3
The Arun - January 2011

According to John

Farming has been the backdrop to our canoeing adventures as well as being our livelihoods. It is a business that, at certain times of year, allows us to disappear for a couple of days while leaving animals and crops in the capable hands of family and staff. I am keen to stress the long hours we put in and the consecutive seven day weeks, for it justifies us in snaching a few days of escape here and there. Fellow canoeists on our expeditions seem to have been other farmers or the unemployed.

Farming has a remarkably low return on capital. That is, very little income is generated from an eye-wateringly expensive asset. As a result of this, many farmers come into the profession via inheritance. We were no different in principle, though my route in was more direct than Martin's.

My father was the youngest of four brothers. When the other three left home, two to other farms and the third to the Air Force and a subsequent career as a butcher, Dad was left with the home farm. I was his only son, so after college I succeeded him to management and title of the land. I believe Martin had hoped to follow a similar plan, but it had not worked out as smoothly for him. On leaving Wye he worked for his father. After a year or two milking cows and helping with the growing of wheat and potatoes, he had found himself managing a nature reserve on the marshes of North Kent. He maintained that his father and he had disagreed severely and it was better to go separate ways. That, too, is a common story in farming families.

After a few years on the nature reserve Martin met Gundrada, who was the youngest of four indomitable sisters. Martin had then proved his father's estimation of his intelligence at least partially wrong by successfully pursuing this lovely girl, with some practical skill and his own version of romance. He was fond of boasting that he finally ran her to ground after a good chase across a potato field on the Romney Marshes. My own view, knowing he was seldom very worldly, is that Gundrada must have given in extremely easily, although she still maintains that she tripped. A farming partnership resulted which under Martin and Gundrada's stewardship grew the small farm into a larger one, during a period that had been difficult for livestock. In the early years, despite being organic, the price of cattle was decimated by the Mad-Cow scare and then the flock caught Foot-and-Mouth disease. Despite such set-backs, family mortgages were re-paid and Montague is now a widely admired demonstration of farming and nature conservation. Somehow he has frustrated conventional economics, tripling the size of his flock when sheep elsewhere were losing money and borrowing money to expand a normally marginal type of farm business. While his father recently expressed a sort of mystified pride in his achievements, I can only comment, after more than 30 years of intimate discussion, that he has a charming ability to live with arrangements that appear largely incomprehensible. He often, modestly, refers to his lovely home as the House of Cards.

Farming in the late twentieth century has revolved around European politics. After the war years food security was seen as vital, but this led to farmers being encouraged to overproduce, which led in turn to the infamous food mountains and milk lakes. This situation was not unique to Britain and one of my favourite books, *Catch 22*, by the American writer Joseph Heller, published in 1961, has brilliantly caught some of the absurdities that have overtaken farming;

> "Major Major's father...was a long limbed farmer, a God-fearing, freedom-loving, law-abiding rugged individualist who... advocated thrift and hard work and disapproved of loose women who turned him down. His speciality was alfalfa, and he made a good thing out of not growing any. The government paid him well for every bushel of alfalfa he did not grow. The more alfalfa he did not grow, the more money the government gave him, and he spent every penny he didn't earn on new land to increase the amount of alfalfa he did not produce. Major Major's father worked without rest at not growing alfalfa. On long winter evenings he remained indoors and did not mend harness, and he sprang out of bed at

the crack of noon every day just to make certain that the chores would not be done. He invested in land wisely and soon was not growing more alfalfa than any other man in the county. Neighbours sought him out for advice on all subjects, for he had made much money and was therefore wise."

Since those days of over production, agricultural policies have sought to encourage sustainability and wildlife friendly farming practices. Some of the policies, such as Set Aside, have been ridiculed. Another Sussex farmer, Stephen Carr, has lampooned the agricultural system, suggesting some imaginative ways by which to reduce farm output. One of my favourites was the "Useless Dog Allowance" (UDA). This involves farmers agreeing to retire their collies and replace them with unsuitable dog breeds in order to scatter the sheep. Martin tells me that Ness would qualify handsomely.

However, truth is always better than fiction, and we came up with our own mechanism for reducing farm output. We called it the "Multiple Birth Incentive" (MBI), payable on the issue of twins or at a higher level for triplets. For both of us this proved most effective and created at least a decade of under-performance. Martin was so good at this that the Royal Society for the Protection of Birds (RSPB) awarded him the UK Lapwing Farmer of the Year accolade as a particularly high number of ground nesting wading birds on Montague marked the first decade of his twin daughters. On my own farm, which has thin chalky soils full of flints, we also opted for organic farming and environmental land management schemes, protecting our chalk stream and creating flower rich pastures on our downland hill-sides. These helped pay the bills, and nature, being best left alone to her ways, delivered the bonus of a bit more free time.

Following our dunking in the Stour the previous January, we had decided to organise ourselves a little better for the expedition on the River Arun. To see what this entailed, (Martin was particularly curious about this), we booked a day out at the Boat Show in London. There we met a man who had canoed down The Yukon and who showed us a film of his remarkable adventure. He kindly advised us of what gear we needed. We left the Boat Show with identical dry bags, life jackets, booties, baboo socks, gloves and helmets. This has caused confusion ever since.

I arrived by car at Arundel train station, on a clear late January afternoon, to await the arrival of Martin and the canoe. His Land Rover had been purchased second hand in 1981. As he entered the station car park the vehicle's age was more apparent than ever. Steam was issuing from the bonnet and I could see a fan belt dangling underneath. Martin was all smiles and greeted me cheerily. Of course he had not noticed the steam, the smell of burning rubber, or the broken fan belt. I had a look at the carnage under the bonnet and diagnosed the problem. Engines not being his forte, he then called the AA. They said they would carry the vehicle back to Montague, but could not fix the broken belts that were the cause of the overheating, so arrangements were made to meet them at Arundel station at five o'clock the following day, after the canoe journey. Meanwhile our logistics for the canoe trip had just got more complicated.

We had planned to put one Land Rover at the river mouth in Littlehampton and leave the other vehicle at Pulborough, where we would launch. This simple plan was now compromised, as Martin's could only travel four miles before overheating and needing a 20 minute rest. He muttered concernedly, wondering how we could complete the trip and return home afterwards. He likes to think of things in a classical way, when he is not banging on about completely irrelevant things. A discussion ensued about the old riddle of the chicken, the fox and the bag of corn, and how to get them across the stream in a boat that could only carry one of them at a time. Martin came up with several ideas, predictably ending with either a temporarily stuffed chicken or a permanently stuffed fox. The simple descent of The Arun now involved two vehicles, only one of which worked, the tide, a liaison with the AA, one canoe, January weather and two farmers.

I tried to put his mind at rest. The chaos he described was not really happening, I suggested. Rather, it is a case of the Heisenberg Uncertainty Principle. The land rover now had a momentum of zero, so there was clearly no way of knowing where it was going to be when we got back. Martin nodded forlornly at this observation and commented that "It can only move if it is towed," pointing at a tow truck in the act of towing away a smart BMW which had been parked illegally. He clearly did not understand Heisenberg's Principle in the slightest and continued to look a little fretful.

Transferring the canoe to the roof of my vehicle, ready for the journey to the launch at Pulborough, we drove separately to the mouth of the river. We left his Land Rover parked in a back-street behind the marina at Littlehampton, ready for the end of the journey on the following afternoon. We inspected the river and its majestic valley as we drove over the Downs to Pulborough to confirm launch arrangements for the morning, and on to The Black Rabbit, a beautiful pub on the river bank, to firm up the lunch arrangements. At Martin's insistence, we popped in to The Wildfowl Trust nature reserve to try and get a view across the floodplain. Unfortunately the river was obscured by prominent flood banks, though we saw good numbers of ducks in the sheltered lagoons, using some binoculars and a powerful telescope provided for visitors in the hide.

Our lodging for the night was the Swan Hotel in the centre of the charming little town of Arundel. Out of politeness we had a drink in the bar, before heading off to discover more about this historic river crossing. The River Arun has an intriguing character. In early times its lower reach was called the Trisantonis, or trespasser, because of a tendency to flood large areas of the majestic valley, and its upper reach was called the Arnus. This caused a rather silly conversation to occur. The mouth of the river has not always been at Littlehampton. Until the later fifteenth century it had crossed eastward to the River Adur, which it joined at Lancing before disgorging into the sea. This estuary then blocked with shingle deposited by the eastward drift of the tide and wind, pushing the Adur east towards Shoreham-by-sea and allowing the Arun to regain independence and break through to the sea at Worthing, then Goring and later at Ferring, before an engineered solution fixed the river mouth at Littlehampton sometime around 1530 AD. The mobility of the river mouth confirmed in my mind that leaving Martin's Land Rover and then rediscovering it may not be as straight forward as I was predicting.

Martin knew a little about Arundel and the cricket ground at the castle. He asserted that the Duke of Norfolk had been a very great cricket fan and that the ground, one of the prettiest in England, once regularly hosted visiting Test teams at the start of their tours. He also described a fixture he had played in at the ground for the Duchess against Cambridge. "Don't ever open the bowling there, it's a batsman's paradise," he advised me. I didn't say that such an invitation was very unlikely, nor did I pursue him with the question of how he got his.

I asked why the Duke of Norfolk had his seat in the middle of Sussex. Martin mumbled something about Catholics, but I could tell he, too, had absolutely no idea. Google is banned on canoe trips, as facts often spoil a good conversation, so we wandered off in search of the answer. The single guest in the first pub was friendly but lacked any knowledge other than the fact that locals were sometimes called mullets. I feared, correctly, that Martin would then deliver a lecture on this fish. Its habit of basking in the brackish river shallows, along with flounder, was then duly expounded upon. When Martin pronounced that the fish was a member of the Mugilidae, the poor man looked insulted, downed his lager and disappeared into the main street.

The second and third pubs yielded as little information and even fewer locals than the first. We wondered if the local from the first pub had warned those in the next two to beware of a pair of loquacious farmers speaking in a strange tongue. The fourth pub yielded some fellow guests, a full history of the Duke and the beautiful Catholic cathedral next to the castle and much other information. The two knowledgeable men with whom we made friends eventually gave their excuses and prepared to leave. Before putting on his coat, one of our new friends gave us a stern warning about The Arun. "It is a powerful river," he advised, "carrying more water to the sea than any other river on the South Coast."

At breakfast the next morning I asked Martin if he knew why the Duke of Norfolk had a seat in the middle of Sussex. He looked confused, muttering that we had better get a move on as high tide was about nine thirty and we had to get to Littlehampton before low tide, and before the AA recovery lorry.

At just after nine thirty we floated away from the medieval arches of the bridge carrying the main road above Pulborough. The water was pushing us up stream, which was definitely not the plan. Martin looked a little sheepish. He now admitted to a slight miscalculation. High tide at Littlehampton was about nine thirty, but the effects of tides up river are very difficult to predict, as it depends on weather, the strength of tide and the amount of water going down the river. On this morning, tidal water was still going up stream and we had clicked for high spring tides. We were to begin our journey paddling against the current, with no option but to push on due to our deadlines at the river mouth. It was raining lightly and Martin, to deflect attention from his organizational miasma, issued a monologue on the shape of rain drops hitting the surface of the river water. He made me listen to the gentle steamy hissing of the water from the sky merging with the water of the river. I almost started to forgive him, for such moments of gentleness are, indeed, precious.

Martin took great pleasure in his own descriptions of nature. He began a story of the Amberley Wildbrooks, an area of superbly wild river marshes which we could see from the canoe. Paddling vigorously, I listened to the story of local people chaining themselves to bulldozers to protect the landscape here from land drainage in the 1970s. He added that he had once been botanising in the area and had chanced upon a Llama, which had expressed surprise by spitting at him. After his tidal miscalculation I had some sympathy with the Llama, but also with his remembered appreciation of the globular pale flowers of the frogbit and an attendant host of china mark moths. The moths, he claimed, were "absolutely unique" in spending the early stages of their life under water. It was an interesting and delicate summer image to set against the leaden skies under which we now laboured, though I did not tell him so. The wildness of the floodplain was exotic, equally now in winter as in summer. January lent a delicious frisson to our paddling.

Below Amberley it seemed that the effects of the tide slowed and then turned. We were starting to make better progress. However, we still had a long way to go, so kept the good pace. We saw what looked like an ordinary duck, but which elicited another rapturous stream of verbage. "A wood duck," he explained, before the inevitable story of its habits and apparent naturalisation in England subsequent to Sir Peter Scott's wetland conservation programmes. Apparently they nest in tall trees in woods and, when the young hatch, the adults kick the little ducklings out of the nest, a sheer 30 foot fall to the ground. I wasn't sure whether such a duck would manage to qualify for the Multiple Birth Incentive of our agricultural imaginings.

Taking on too much fluid is a mistake on a canoe trip. A wet suit with a number of layers over it, to keep out the January cold, takes quite a lot of removing. We eventually could bear it no longer. The combined impact of last night's pub crawl and this morning's attempt at rehydration could no longer be ignored. We pulled up on the edge of the river, taking off coats and fumbling with neoprene and body length zips as we went, ignoring the flurry of wings from a large flight of ducks as we breasted the flood banks. It was not until we had both finished relieving ourselves that we were able to take in our surroundings. From the vantage of the top of the flood banks we had an excellent view into the hides of the Wildfowl Trust nature reserve. From the hides the view would have been less excellent. Two hairy farmers missing most of their clothes and urinating happily as all the ducks disappeared. And to think they would have binoculars and telescopes..... We hurriedly re-dressed and returned to our mission.

Arundel castle appeared on the horizon. It is a magnificent and beautiful building, with ranks of dramatic towers and ramparts giving it a powerful presence over the wild river valley. I had a sudden recollection of our conversation in the fourth pub last night. Built nearly a thousand years ago, after the Norman invasion, it became the seat of the noble Howards in the 16th century. The third Duke of Norfolk had been the uncle of two of the wives of Henry VIII, Anne Boleyn and Catherine Howard. His son, the fourth Duke, had then married the female heir to Arundel castle, Mary FitzAlan, which is how the Norfolks came to Sussex. Martin, after commenting on what a sensible marriage the fourth Duke had made, then added that a lot of the castle was restored in the 19th century, by the Drunken Duke, who was a crony of the Prince Regent. He rambled on, telling me that he had been brought up farming on land belonging to the Viscount Hampden, who had told him one day that no Hampden had been to Arundel since the offer to remove an ancestor's head from his shoulders had been made by the Howards, who were fighting for the Royalists against the Cromwellian Hampdens, in the English Civil War. Our memories had finally recovered.

The river meandered in graceful loops. Looking up we were able to see the dominating castle in its winter glory, as the weak sun had replaced the drizzle. The meanders were interesting too, with the westward outward bends cutting into exposed chalk creating exotic white river cliffs, some of which had also been quarried. Some meanders were overhung with mixed woodland, dominated by yew trees. There was a forest nearby, said Martin, called Kingley Vale, where ancient yews grew, some of which were thought to be over 4000 years old, ten times the age assumed in all the literature. Unfortunately yews of that age tend to have rotted from the middle, so information gathered from tree rings or from carbon dating is fraught with the problem that the oldest part of the tree is no longer evident. For that reason, it was very hard to establish the exact age of the trees, so nobody actually knew how old they were.

I reminded him that the creosote bushes of the Mojave Desert could be more than 11000 years old, the oldest being King Clone, which was dated at 11700 years. I had learnt this from Stephen Fry on his Quiz programme, QI, but it was seldom that the many facts I had assembled from the tv programme came in useful. Martin was surprised at my tree knowledge.

I also thought that, though our conversation seemed escapist, it was simply a reflection from a different angle, afforded by being on the river. After all, the South Downs are a mirror image of the North Downs, where I farm and we too have ancient yews. Martin's mention of Cromwell also chimed with home, as during a campaign in the Civil War Cromwell had once hidden his New Model army in the cellar beneath our farm house. Martin knew this history, but still insisted on asking if the soldiers were real or whether it was a "model New Model Army" that had visited the cellar. He had a habit of laughing at his own jokes and chuckled away while he paddled.

When we canoed the Cuckmere, which also cut through the South Downs, Martin had begun a lecture on the formation of chalk. He continued now, interrupting my musings with talk about warm seas 60 million years ago and huge populations of single celled organisms whose bodies piled up on the ancient sea bed to create this fascinating rock. The most prolific of these creatures was called Emiliania huxleyi, after the two great scientists who early got to grips with a modern microscope. I was amused to learn that this tiny phytoplankton, when blooming, was visible from the moon. It was still having an impact on the ecology of the Earth, yet singly could not be seen by the eye of man. Martin loved to pronounce these Latin names with a sort of reverential expressiveness. He was prone to do the same with the names of French rugger players, if you happened to be watching rugby with him, repeating the names Pascal Pappe and Papparambert in a sort of energetic, dramatised growl.

We knew that we were on the bends that passed the Black Rabbit, where a delicious lunch would be available. It had been a strenuous morning. I was looking forward to a comfortable chair by the fire with a plate of hot food in front of me.

"Can't stop," said Martin. He was right. We had lost time at the top of the river, paddling against the tidal current and had only two hours in which to get to Littlehampton before the tide once again turned. We looked at the elegant veranda as we passed, ruing the currents controlling our day. Lunch was a Mars Bar on the bridge in Arundel, as we passed through the town once again. Our muscles were starting to complain as we continued towards our destination.

The river character changes again below the town, as the marshes open out onto the coastal plain where the river is entirely tidal in nature. Energised by the smell of the sea and the sight of the sprawl of Littlehampton, we pushed our tired bodies onward. This journey had been very hard work. At exactly 3.30, two minutes before low tide and the consequent turn of the river current, we hit the waves of the English Channel.

Martin, however, was not looking very pleased. We had passed his Land Rover about half a mile back and I had insisted we could not stop until reaching the sea. We stood on the shingle beach. Usually such moments are triumphal.

"We have less than one hour to get my Land Rover, stow the canoe and drive four miles to Arundel, before the AA get there." With that he disappeared briskly in the direction of where he claimed to remember having parked. An eternity passed before a heat haze appeared near the entrance to the car park where I had dragged the canoe. Martin had got lost in the one way system, used up his four mile range, overheated the engine and then overheated himself, judging by the look on his face.

He is usually an easy-going, genial sort of a person, but he had admitted to me during the trip that a couple of incidents had occurred recently which had ended up in some unusually colourful language, "the sort usually reserved for the instruction of the collies." Whatever was wrong with him seemed to have resurfaced and he was really pretty cross that we had not stopped before the sea in order to collect the injured vehicle, clearly panicking about not getting on the recovery truck. I shrugged, already relishing the prospect of describing the situation at the next gathering of the Wye Rustics. That thought put in train another recollection, of Martin being regularly unravelled in a cricket match we played at Kilmington, a village near Axminster in Devon.

Kilmington is our longest standing fixture of the tour. It is a charming little ground, overlooked by the church and with a magnificent pine tree in one corner. The muscular farmers in our team have caused much damage there, breaking windows, roof tiles, benches and cars with their big hitting. In the 1980s the village had two feared fast bowlers, in Messers Sturch and Rocket, and the fixture was a tough contest. These days we line up against their grand-sons, with a little less fear. With Martin's ability to hit the ball miles he relishes batting there. Kilmington however have a secret weapon, a small, balding retired shopkeeper. He is a slow somewhat ineffective bowler, and I too have enjoyed hitting his loopy little bowling to all parts of the ground. He has an odd run up and at the start of it the Rustics will turn as one to watch Martin, wherever he is, but especially if he is batting. He twitches irritably and froths incoherently. He is like a hungry bear being attacked by a swarm of bees. His usual poise and affability evaporates, even if he is only watching from the boundary. This nemesis goes by the name of James Kirkaldy. He starts his approach to bowl by theatrically hitching his ill fitting trousers, then re-rolling the sleeves on his equally ill-fitting shirt, exhibiting signs of some peculiar neurosis. Next, he adjusts his little round spectacles, held on his head by an elastic band. Flat footed, he somehow manages a skip and a shuffle before delivering the ball at an impossibly slow pace. If Martin is batting then what happens next is a foregone conclusion. He is clean bowled or out, stumped, having taken the most almighty swish at the elusive ball. As Kircaldy is even older than us, this pantomime has been going on for nearly 30 years.

The usual kerfuffle of strapping the canoe to the roof allowed Martin and the vehicle to cool down. He was very particular about this operation. We are used to being in charge of our own businesses and have both developed streaks of autocracy that probably make us un-employable. This proves itself in the habitual failure to co-operate at the different ends of the ropes and the newly acquired ratchet straps. This is my chapter, and I contend that Martin has not the foggiest idea how a ratchet strap actually works. It is also an enduring mystery how he manages to tie the canoe on so that when any speed above 40 mph is reached the ropes and straps achieve a hideous whirring vibration that drowns out all other noise.

A nervy return to Arundel was successfully undertaken despite a nasty moment when temperatures soared as we waited for a train at a level crossing. We made contact with the AA recovery truck, which was also exactly on time, and I left to board a train in order to collect my land rover from Pulborough. As it pulled out of the station to wend its way up the Arun valley, I leant out of the window to wave goodbye. The truck passed the train but Martin had already fallen asleep in the passenger seat, his canoe strapped firmly to the green Land Rover, in turn chained to the recovery truck. The load looked most eccentric.

Chapter 4
The Two Rivers of Tarka the Otter - January 2012

By Martin

Two winters after the epic descent of the Stour I came up with a plan to do the Tamar. This river separates Devon from Cornwall and cuts through some wonderful countryside. As a January paddle from source to sea it would be a great adventure, and so it remains. A quixotic change of mind, if not county, and we assembled a team to enjoy the two Rivers of the otter immortalised in Henry Williamson's "*Tarka the Otter,*" the Taw and the Torridge. To this day I do not understand why we did not do The Tamar, but it turned out to be a great decision.

We planned this time to take both canoes and two men in addition to John and I. Two two-man canoes, we had decided, would be a more social adventure and someone had once mentioned to me that multiple canoes might also be a safer strategy, especially negotiating white-water. Naturally, we would disprove the second assertion, but the first part was definitely right.

The week before we were due to head down towards Exmoor John phoned me.

"Great news," he said, "Simon also said yes."

"Who is Simon?" I asked, a little confused. "Is he coming instead of Gavin or George?"

"No, it's brilliant. They have all said yes. So that makes four."

I went slightly quiet.

"Well, and you, of course," said John. "That makes five…"

John loved mathematical conundrums, he even sort of understood quantum physics and could talk free radicals with anyone who cared to listen. However, he seemed to have missed the basic maths of the adventure founded on two two-man canoes. George, who I had met once before, did not weigh much. I just hoped that Gavin and Simon, whom I had not met before, were equally svelte fellows.

The night before we were due to tackle the waters of the Taw, we gathered at George's farm in Dorset. Here I met Gavin and Simon for the first time. Canoeing is an intimate pastime, so I studied the new crew carefully. Simon seemed both quiet and charming. An expert skier, he had filmed ski sports for television. He was an ocean going yachtsman with his own sailing boat, and a good hockey player to boot. I looked forward to learning more about him. He only had two days for the river adventure as he had to attend a television awards evening in London in case he had won one of the prizes. Gavin looked a bit more tousled and was into corporate information technology, not a good start, but I looked him frankly in the eye and was pleased to see an expression of both deep kindness and great humour. This first impression was wholly and delightfully correct. He was one of John's hockey friends and in fact George also played hockey, for a local veterans eleven in Dorset. Our adventures appeared to answer the "After Cricket" question for hockey also. Gavin and Simon were similar sized and definitely not overweight. Nor were they especially small. I thought that so long as John and I were not two of a three man crew we might get down the river with one of the canoes containing three men.

George's farm is an impressive operation. Beautifully managed by him and his brother, the immaculate crops are bounded by wonderful hedges, beside woods and pastures full of wildflowers. If a man's farm can reflect his soul, then George must be beautiful and well structured on the inside. More importantly, the farm is near the brewery outside Blandford Forum. We sampled some of the local fare and had a companionable evening getting to know one another and firming up our plans for the adventure. In particular, who had what "special subject."

Simon had prepared a dissertation on bees and Gavin on the political upheavals in North Africa, as he had once worked in Libya. John had given his topic the title "Fearful Symmetry," and George was going to explain to us how many times you can fold a piece of paper. (I believe the answer is seven, but I do not recall the number clearly.) All four of us sniggered slightly when George revealed his topic. He looked hurt, so we gave him slack and looked forward to the time when all would be revealed. My own role was to guide the adventure on the two rivers in the footsteps of Tarka the Otter, relating as we paddled the events of the otter's life. Given my love of this book I rather felt that my companions were in for a treat.

The two rivers rise close to one another on Dartmoor, on Taw marsh between Cranmere Tarn and Cawsand Beacon. The Taw heads slightly west north-west through the granite gully of the Belstone Cleave and is joined by waters off Exmoor before disgorging into the estuary it shares with the Torridge at Barnstaple. The Torridge heads more due west, south of the Taw, beginning life as the river Oakment before joining waters from Bodmin Moor when it becomes the Torridge proper. It also then cuts through the hard rock of the ancient, carboniferous downfold, called the Culm synclinorium by geologists, before getting to the North Devon coast. The eventful life of Tarka was played out graphically amongst this variety of seasons and of rock and river, coast and moor.

In the small dark hours of the morning we left George's home, which has the entirely appropriate name of Traveller's Rest Farm, in two vehicles. A hard frost still gripped the night and the land we crossed. We drove west in the dark. After breakfast at a farm shop one vehicle was parked at Umberleigh station and the other driven about 15 miles up-river, with the canoes. We eventually found a suitable launch point. In addition to finding somewhere to park and enter the river I was keen to find an old tree. The River Taw was lined with a gallery forest of trees, dripping with mosses, and I especially sought a large oak tree. It was in the roots of such a riverside giant, fallen in a previous winter, that Tarka's life began. The tree was described thus in the book:

" ... the oak nearest the North Star had never thriven, since first a pale green hook had pushed out of a swelled black acorn left by floods on the bank more than three centuries before. In its second year a bullock's hoof had crushed the seedling, breaking its two ruddy leaves, and the sapling grew up crooked. The cleft of its fork held the rain of two hundred years, until frost made a wedge of ice that split the trunk; another century's weather wore it hollow, while every flood took more earth and stones from under it. And one rainy night, when salmon and peal from the sea were swimming against the brown rushing water, the tree had suddenly groaned...."

Standing by the edge of the Taw I introduced the crew to the river with this passage. I explained that we were entering an ancient and dynamic landscape, as if into another dimension. This was a parallel world where the lives of nature's cast were made tangible, the one in which Tarka lived his life.

"Who's coming with me?" said John. So captivated by the hurrying current of The Taw, the clear water and the trees leaning over to protect the inner sanctum of the river course, I had neglected to make a plan. John gained a huge advantage for the journey. His query actually meant that I was to be saddled with the three-man canoe. By default Gavin and Simon were assigned to me and it was at this moment that I discovered neither had been on a canoe expedition before.

After a safety talk consisting of the single piece of advice to "not fall in," we pushed off from the gnarly tree roots forming our launch site. The river was swift and rocky, with short runs of white-riffling water. The frost still hung about and the sky was overcast. For January it was a good day. We passed under a lovely old sandstone bridge, opting for the left-hand arch. The river turned playfully below its reach. I was transported mentally to another plane, so beautiful was our setting and so excited was I to be in Tarka's world.

We saw a kingfisher and then some dippers which, I explained to my crew, feed in the river by angling their tail feathers so that the moving water kept them pressed to the bed where they could catch their feed. These creatures were joined by a sandpiper, wings bent, gliding away from us low over the water. We heard the chatter of the river spirit birds, the grey wagtails, before catching sight of them.

We are a generation who grew up in a world where otters had been driven to near extinction. Hunting otters with hounds stopped in the 1970s, as the population was cruelly decimated by the pollution of its water and food chain, in particular by organo-chlorides. The last 40 years have seen the withdrawal of these chemicals and a widespread clean up of our rivers and their margins. Otters now breed in nearly all parts of England again, especially in these West Country rivers. A recent survey had shown them to have re-colonised nearly all of the English counties, with Sussex curiously among the exceptions. Their revival was a conservation success, which meant we might even be lucky enough to see one.

Above us a buzzard flew from the woodland that blanketed the steep escarpment of the river valley. I remembered that the buzzard was referred to as the "mewliboy" in the book, which is adorned by colourful vocabulary and many vernacular words. I told Simon, as he was fascinated by insects, that there was a special descriptor, "appledrane," for the sound of a wasp buzzing in the carcase of a rotting apple.

We were approaching the Junction Pool. I thought that this place, which does feature in the story, was where Tarka had a rather exciting tryst with an older, more experienced she otter. At least I felt this was the time to relate the details of the coupling, even if it had not actually taken place in the pool. I embarked on a lascivious account of their love-making, set in the spring moonlight and with their noisy, care-free, passion-fuelled "yikkering." I surpassed myself with a description of the torrid ottery romance.

The Junction Pool loomed. It is where the River Mole, bringing water from Exmoor, joins the Taw. The Mole brings a lot of water from Exmoor, especially in January. The pool is deceptive, appearing at first as just that, really a gentle widening of the river. Fringed with reed and fallen willows, it is a secret expanse of water where the river momentarily becomes a quiet lake with swampy hinterlands. John had already passed this way, some distance ahead of the three of us. I was still stuck in a thrall of imagined, highly verbalised, otter action.

At the end of the pool the river, having been joined by the Mole's much greater volume of water, became a destructive torrent. The powerful thrust of the water heading out of the pool charged straight into a large earth cliff, which it was quite dramatically undercutting, on the outside of a very sharp bend.

Receiving no advice from me at the back of the canoe, Simon and Gavin carried on paddling. I had forgotten that they were novices. I tried to steer, but that proved impossible. Three men all doing something different did not help, nor the fact that the canoe had very little freeboard, as a result of the weight of its occupants. The current in which we were caught was a destructive surge throwing itself, and the canoe, hungrily at the mud cliff.

A last effort to steer failed completely. The boat flooded and turned over as it was rammed into the face of the muddy precipice. On entering the freezing fast-running water I felt just like the baby Tarka when he first swam in the river;

> "...he dropped down into the black, star-shivery water. He was clutched in a cold and terrible embrace, so that he could neither see nor breathe, and although he tried to walk, it smothered him, choked him, roared in his ears, and stifled every mew for help..."

I did not surface immediately. Nor could I find the bottom of the river. I was reminded later that I had informed our guests that the river was seldom more than chest deep. The scouring action of the redoubled water must have etched a deep channel, in which we were now tumbling along beneath the surface. It could have been 20 feet deep, as none of us managed to touch the bottom.

I was the first to surface. I had a life jacket. I had lent a second life jacket to Gavin. He had surfaced, unknown to me, but had come up into the upside down canoe. I did not know where he was. I now thought I was party to a shocking tragedy involving two drowned men. I had visions of the inquest.

"Mr Hole, please tell the court what you, the only experienced canoeist in the boat, were doing prior to this accident?"

"Well, Your Honour, I was describing the sex life of an otter ..."

Gavin then bobbed up beside the boat, having extricated himself from the upturned hulk, looking a little shocked. Horribly, our joint realisation was that we had been swept at least 100 metres below the Junction Pool, still travelling briskly, and there was no sign of Simon. He could be anywhere, trapped under a tree or face down under the turbulent water.

A moment later there was an exploding noise and a blur of colour. Simon had eschewed my offer of an old lifejacket, instead donning the latest yachtie lifesaver. The exploding life vest had eventually gone off and probably saved his life, but it did not save his dignity. He had not simply bobbed to the surface, but had emerged from the water like a sea to air ballistic missile. Only at this moment was laughter the order of the day, with nothing lost other than a bit of pride.... and Gavin's hat.

We emptied the water from the boat and re composed ourselves on the river, swiftly descending to where John and George had moored, and from where George had got some really good photographs of our upset. They were shouting excitedly to us as we set in to the bank, another manoeuvre of which we managed to make a hash, for not only had they had a grandstand view of our capsize, but they had actually seen an otter.

"Well, at least we've all been an otter," I harrumphed, disappointed that I had missed such a sighting. I glanced at George. He still looked immaculate in his brand new green and blue dry suit. He tried to look sympathetic for the plight of the three drowned rats in front of him. He gave up, smiled wickedly and took another photograph. We then consulted the map. On it there was a pub marked, which we had seen beforehand and where we hoped to get lunch. We were cold, wet and hungry, though thankful for our wet suits. We hurried back onto the river and down to where we knew we could find a nice warm bar and some lunch.

It had been a good plan. The pub was located roughly half way along our route and close to the river. Unfortunately we discovered, as we stood outside its locked doors, that it was closed for the whole of January for refurbishment. The Portsmouth Arms would not be able to embrace our party, but all was not lost. A sign on the other side of the road stated "Northcote Manor, five star hotel, one and a half miles."

Having hidden the canoes by the Taw, the four middle aged men in wet suits and one in an elaborate colourful dry suit then set off along the road. It certainly felt eccentric, though thankfully we were in a very rural area with no traffic. The flat road followed the river valley. After a mile and a half, during which we had passed only farms and isolated cottages, we came to the stone pillars at the entrance to Northcote Manor's drive. I think I already mentioned that we were cold and hungry, and that three of us were still wet. In fact, the walk was not particularly chatty, squelches easily out-numbering words.

"Aaah," said John, using the word he reserved for satisfying moments, "Lunch beckons."

The drive was another mile of walking, climbing the whole way up a very steep hill. Eventually the hotel appeared in front of us. A grand manor house with commanding views and beautiful grounds, it looked very five star indeed. Having walked so far, we were now in a dilemma.

"They will never let us in," said George.

"It will be shut," said Simon, having assimilated the pessimism we farmers normally reserved for forecasts.

Gavin knocked on the big oak door, which was opened very quickly by the smartly suited Maitre d'. He hid his surprise beautifully and, much to our amazement, ushered us into the gloriously warm and elegant entrance hall. We left puddles and our paddles by the door and squelched gratefully onto the Persian rug, creating another puddle in front of the wood burner. We stood there guiltily, not daring to sit on the leather sofa. There was no sign of any other guests, the car park had been empty and not much happened in deepest Devon in January. It slowly dawned that they might even be pleased to see us. Incredibly, the Maitre d' invited us to sit. Gavin muttered that maybe we had died on the river, after all, and now we were in heaven. We sat on the leather sofa and countered his observation with the fact that neither John nor George would still be with us if that were the case.

We ordered sandwiches which quickly came. Real bread and rare roast beef, smoked salmon and proper egg mixture. Our spirits revived. Though it was raw January outside, and now raining, I thought a little bit of Tarka was appropriate. After Tarka's moonlit activities in the Junction Pool he, too, had felt hungry. He had attacked an old Eel, one eyed after being snagged by a fishing hook that was still embedded in the Eel's now empty eye socket.

> "The eel was longer than Tarka. It lashed its tail round his neck and bit on to his nose, when gripped below the paired fins. Bubbles were blown in two strings, one of them fine as charlock seeds, for the hook shank was rammed up the otter's left nostril. Then the strings ceased, and stray bubbles arose, for the eel was throttling the otter.....For three minutes until his breath was gone, he tried to shake off the eel. Then he kicked heavily and slowly up to the surface and tried to climb out by the nearest land - a sheer bank..."

Our long walk had been a comparable effort to fighting such an Eel, we all agreed.

"I've got a great idea. Let's stay here for our second night," said John. The four of us blanched at perceived expenditure, but a robust negotiation then ensued. Gavin took charge. After some time Gavin came back to us with the news that he had got a really good deal, luxury rooms for each of us for half the normal rate. In fact, no different to the rate we were paying at the Rising Sun. On leaving the hotel we all noticed an advert by the door offering a midweek stay during January for half price, exactly what Gavin had claimed to have won through his shrewd bargaining.... We booked our rooms for the second night with great pleasure, before venturing once more into the Devon countryside for the return walk to where we had stowed the canoes.

Paddling into the late afternoon, we arrived at Umberleigh in the dark and got out of the river by the old mill. An ancient, buttery-stone building which had recently been re-thatched, it resembled the mill in which Tarka had hidden in the mill-wheel from the hounds while eluding Deadlock in the great hunt, and at which the huntsmen had also rested during their lunch.

The Rising Sun at Umberleigh is a famous Devon pub much frequented by countrymen, often after shooting, fishing or hunting. It was because a shooting party were in occupation that we were not able to get beds there for our second night and the reason why we had booked at the Manor.

Showered and changed, we gathered for dinner. I had a steak, but John had duck. His choice was excellent, and I declared intent to return the next day to partake of some myself. Then as the evening progressed, we decided it was time for special subjects. Simon gave us a very detailed insight into the life of the honey bee. We were ready, of course, to make his life difficult, and attacked him on his description of the "waggle dance," whereby the bee shows its fellow workers the route to a nectar source. Being a modest man, he declined to give us an imitation of the dance, but quelled us with some surprising new information on the subject. Bees do not simply buzz. Researchers at the University of Munich have apparently recorded a low frequency hum of exotic ululation made by the bee during its performance of the waggle. The Queen Bee has also been recorded making piping and hooting sounds when confronting a rival. Other sounds included the noise of the bee's feet when walking across the honeycomb. Our imagining of the bee cacophony replaced our teasing of Simon, who thus completed his exposition. Latterly, I have heard the above-mentioned noises set to music, the Queen re-created by the notes of a cello.

Gavin's turn was next, and he gave us a history lesson on Libya. The standard had been set high by the depth of knowledge revealed by Simon, but, as ever, Gavin came up with the goods. He had worked in Libya for several years and had some exciting experiences with which he peppered his description of North African history. One of these involved a midnight escape from his lodgings to escape a threatened kidnap attempt. This left only the two other farmers to give their special subject. They agreed to wait until the following night. We had The Torridge River to descend on the following day and so, in preparation, went to bed when the bar shut.

The weather was cold and raining gently when we loaded the canoes the following morning. As we searched for the best place to leave our vehicle and enter the river, I told our assembled crew of Tarka's Great Winter, when he had fled to the estuary in search of food:

> "The ice-talons set harder in the land. No twitter of finch or linnet was heard on the Burrows for those which remained were dead.....Even crows died of starvation.....The wind whined in the skeleton of his mate, broken at the knees, near the skull of Marland Jimmy gaping at the crown, eyeless and showing its teeth in the ice."

The scene of cataclysmic cold is adorned by the arrival of Bubu, the Arctic owl, a murderer blown south on the ferocious winds. He tries to scavenge from one of Tarka's kills, a bloodied mute swan.

> "....he reached the conflict, fanning above like a shade of chaos,....staring like the Northern Lights, taloned like black frost."

The otters manage to survive, but the winter is brutal. This evocation of

Winter is one of the most powerful in all literature. It gave us a reminder of why canoeing in January can be such a great adventure. I am still on a roll as we launch the canoes some 10 miles from Torrington. Once again there are three men in my boat, but the Torridge is, if anything, even more beautiful than the Taw and we canoed happily and without any mishap down to Torrington for lunch.

Predictably, given our history of botched lunch venues, the pub by the river was also shut for the whole of January. We were cold and hungry, as we had been the day before, so we hid the canoes in the old glass factory, once the site of the manufacture of the world famous Dartington crystal, and again went for a long walk up a hill, this time through a busy town centre. I did not understand the looks we received, until I glanced at my companions. Our band of wet-suited men, and George, did cut an odd sight in this little Devon town.

After lunch we completed our journey to the start of the estuary, but stopped short of the sea, despite John's on-going insistence that we had not completed the river until we were rocking in the waves. I had managed to complete my special subject by giving the crew a graphic taste of Tarka's final long and drawn out battle with the great hound, his mortal enemy, Deadlock.

That night we stayed at the luxurious country house hotel, Northcote Manor, but dined at the Rising Sun, which was a few miles up the road and required us to arrange a taxi. My reason for going there was to enjoy a dish of the duck which John had eaten the night before. Consistent with the culinary disappointment which has afflicted this adventure, I discovered, on arrival at the pub, that the duck was off the menu!

Simon had hurried off to London to his awards dinner, where unfortunately he did not win any of the awards. The event was televised and viewable in a back bar. There was some unkind chortling amongst ourselves, for when the cameras panned to his table he looked distinctly as if he were having a little nap. Afterwards we suffered George's special subject, on folding a napkin. Somehow though it started us giggling, so John's epic presentation concerning "Fearful symmetry and the work at Cerne" got no further than William Blake's famous verse from *The Tiger*:

"Tiger, Tiger, burning bright, in the forests of the night, what immortal hand or eye, could frame thy fearful symmetry."

Chapter 5
The Wye - A family holiday - July 2012

By Martin

Our trip to the London Boat Show earlier in the year had given John and I the wonderful idea of a Hole and Dinnis family holiday, canoeing down the River Wye and staying in Red Indian wigwams. It would be a perfect adventure for the full complement of the combined Iceni. The major selling point to Julie and Gundrada was the promise that the camping would be fully catered for by the tour company. The camps would have decent loos and hot showers, and it would be a complete break for them both. As for the canoeing, that would be a doddle in the swift and swirling flat waters of the lovely river, so rest was assured.

The river Wye rises at over 2000 feet, high in the Cambrian mountains of Wales, at Plynlimon, not far from the source of the Severn, and cuts its way through the Welsh border lands to emerge in The Severn Estuary at Chepstow. It eases its journey through Powys, Herefordshire, Monmouthshire and Gloucestershire, among varied and pretty countryside rich in wildlife, through historic towns and past archaeological treasures. The river is wide and graceful on the stretch below Hereford, and the removal of the weirs in the 17th Century meant that the unobstructed waters were safe to paddle and ideally suited for our boats loaded with children. The oldest of these were Florence and Poppy, aged 14, closely followed by George, 13, and his friend James, then Romney, aged 12 then Rosie, Hattie and Issie measuring 11. That made eight children and four adults, or in the reckoning of our wives ten children and two adults.

It was a long journey from Montague to Hereford and to stave off the inevitable "Are we nearly there, yet?" question, which my three had converted into a song garnered from a school play, we played a natural history knowledge game. Florence did well getting lapwing for Vanellus vanellus, and Poppy did equally well with green winged orchid for Orchis morio, a plant that grew prolifically in our hay meadows at home. "What is Gyrinus gyrinator?" I asked Romney, choosing this most comic beetle because it was common in our ditches and ponds, whirring in circles on the clean water. A slight delay followed, then the correct answer, "a whirly-gig beetle, Dad."

Sensing conspiracy, I glanced into the rear view mirror and as I had suspected, Romney's head was buried in her telephone. I tried a different line of questioning. "Where in the country is the approximate divide between the sessile and the pedunculate oak?" A hive of industry on the back seat as the twins now also bent over Romney's phone. "Sessile oaks are found mainly in the north and west of Britain," came the reply. "What does that mean we will see in Herefordshire?" Florence, with no phone, got the answer first. "See, sometimes you don't need a phone," I crowed at Pops and Rom.

Having nagged Romney and Poppy interminably about not continuously looking at their telephones, I now was rather pleased at the girls' access to its information. My most recent question had bought back the Wikipedia entry on the river, from which Romney read out a brief account of the salmon population in the Wye;

> "Once famous for its salmon fishing, the catch has dwindled in recent years, from over 7000 caught by rod in 1967 to just 357 in 2002. The river was particularly famed for large "spring" salmon, fish that have spent three or more years at sea before returning to spawn, the largest being 59 pounds and 8 ounces, landed after a long fight by Miss Doreen Davey from the Cowpond pool at Ballingham on 13th March 1923. The last 50 pounder to be caught was in 1963, with no fish of comparable weight caught in any of the years since."

Gundrada, who had been quiet for a while, then suggested we had a round of the guessing game, in which each of our turns began "I'm a little animal and I begin with..." then adding the first letter of the creature's name. She always chose furry and smelly mustelids, of which she had an amazing and diverse knowledge. Whatever letter she chose, the children would usually shout "ferret."

We arrived at the campsite in the early evening, at exactly the same time as the Dinnissiae. My three girls instantly disappeared with his three, followed at only a slight distance by George and his friend James, creating a little war-party. We had three wigwams between us and the whole site entirely to ourselves, largely because we had taken the children out of school two days before the official end of term. We were right beside the river, both the setting and the weather were perfect.

We were greeted by a team of young helpers, who carried our luggage to the exotic looking tents, and then left. The bit I was hoping for didn't seem to be happening: there was no cook, nor any sign of a cooking facility other than a rather damp looking fire pit. It looked as if it woould take a week to heat up, although that was pure fancy as I had not bought anything to eat let alone barbeque. My attempt to light a fire inside the wigwam did not go well either. A complex system of flaps and long poles gave me a graphic insight as to why Red Indians communicated with smoke signals and liked living outdoors. I retreated from the tent feeling rather defeated and with streaming eyes.

Julie and Gundrada had wandered off to look at the river. I had only a moment to come up with something, with regards to food, and included John in this duty. "Remember, John, we promised our wives that they would not have to worry about a thing. Catering would all be taken care of. I'm afraid I didn't bring a bean." I said quietly but rather anxiously.

"Hmmm," said John, really quite irritatingly, considering the impending state of emergency. He wandered off with his nose in his telephone. I looked around for some inspiration. There was none to be had and I had the feeling I was only a minute or two away from eight very hungry children and two very angry wives. I began to feel like a solitary man on a desert island facing a tribe of cannibals, contemplating his role as the main course, or like Caesar fearing battle with Boadicea.

Then John returned. He lifted up his smart telephone, which I could not decipher as my reading glasses were in my dry bag. The bag had been put in the smoky wigwam where Gundrada was organising beds, having returned from her walk on the river side. I wasn't going over there for all the tea in China. Her first comment would be something like "tricky things, these wigwam fires," and her first question would be, "do you think it's time for the children's meal?" I had a fearful vision of me trussed to a spit over the charcoal pit, being slow roasted to feed our hungry families. I was desperate. "Look at it, you fool," John persisted, interrupting my miserable reverie. Eventually, John read out what was on the infernal screen: "Reservation for twelve confirmed for seven o'clock." I surprised myself by discovering that one could actually love a smart phone, and worse I believe I may have even given John a hug.

I sauntered over to the wigwam, from which the smoke had nearly cleared. Not since my honeymoon had I advanced towards my wife with such self-assurance, swaggering euphorically in my recently assumed mantle of the all-providing male.

"We'd better hurry, darling, dinner will be ready in half an hour," I said with an insouciance I had not thought possible two minutes before.

We had a terrific meal in a nearby pub. The conversation was noisy and full of excitement about the forthcoming trip down this beautiful river. After a couple of pints of ale and animated discussion of the adventure ahead of us, I relaxed enough to regale the adults of our party with a discovery I had made concerning Latin names, from a book called *The Naming of the Shrew*. A species of mould, Cucurbitaria applanata, had been named in collaboration between two German mycologists, Otto Kuntze and Leopold Fuckel, and in formal scientific papers the species could be followed by a four letter abbreviation of each of the discoverer's names. Non-English-speaking taxonomists had proceeded with abbreviation and thus created an unspeakable double.

That night was interrupted by an unfortunate event. Gundrada and I were in one tent, John and Julie in another tent and all of the children voluntarily together in the third. Sometime in the small hours John had pushed, sleepily, through our tent flap and settled on to one of the spare beds.

"I've been sent to sleep with Martin," he said, crashing out on a spare futon and promptly re-commencing his snoring.

"I'm sleeping with Julie," said Gundrada, and, equally promptly, disappeared. It marked the end of any prospect of holiday romance between Boadicea and her charioteer.

In the morning, after a panic food buying expedition to a Hereford supermarket which had replaced the plan of looking at the Mappa Mundi in Hereford Cathedral, we departed the town in four canoes. The luggage and all the shopping was transported to the next camp site by our hosts. It was a joy to finally feel the Wye chuckling beneath the thin bottom of the canoe.

I had Hattie, Issie and Romney in my boat. The first instructions I offered to them, with regard to paddling, was that the river should be treated with respect and, in particular, there should be no splashing of other paddlers. Within a millisecond of purveying this thought to my crew I was completely soaked. I took no retaliatory action, because Issie and Hattie had the nuclear option still up their sleeve. They could call on Rosie. I knew that a combined assault from all three was more than I could repel. We paddled on. In fact, while I am thinking about it, that is not quite true. After the first few hundred yards, I paddled on as the three girls in my boat dangled their arms over the side and lay back gossiping about all matters pony. The journey looked like it would be harder work than I had predicted.

The day was warm and the surface of the water glistened in dancing shards of sunlight, as the river flowed busily onwards. I dried out in a few minutes and tried to point out a few creatures of the river to the children. They would not believe me when I pointed at a grey wagtail, because it was bright yellow. Dragonflies were only briefly interesting to them, as I shirked the facts of life by suggesting that they would carry one another along while in flight, and when I pointed to a type of duck called a goosander I was immediately mocked by my passengers. Hattie mimicked my voice, announcing the bird as "so called because it goos under the water to feed..." Clearly, I had my work cut out in more ways than one, so did not venture the information I had gleaned from an ecological survey about the depressed river mussel and the horny orb snail, both of which could be found in the waters of the Wye.

The babble of happy children merged with the merry murmur of the river. I mused, to myself mainly, about halcyon days. Days of peace and beauty were granted to Alcyone, a woman from a Greek myth, in order to help her locate her husband who had been lost at sea. Such "halcyon days" also came to represent a period of calm weather at the time a kingfisher nested, assumed wrongly by the Greeks to be a week either side of the winter solstice. Today we use the expression to describe the days of warm summer that honey our understanding of youth. It is this context in which I enjoyed the phrase on this glorious morning.

The Halcyon is also a name given to the kingfisher, a bird we were seeing a lot on the river. At this time of year they were frantically feeding their large broods, being July it would be their second, which could number up to seven in a normal nest. A successful pair of kingfishers could thus theoretically raise twelve to fifteen young in a single year. I looked across at the number of children happily not paddling in our canoes and admired the parental energy of these vigorous and very colourful fisher birds. I restricted my observations to simply pointing them out to the girls, who did seem more interested in this jewel than the many others we were passing.

After a pub lunch and another long journey in the afternoon on the Wye, we were delighted to see the campsite. There were three wigwams and yet again we had the site entirely to ourselves, perfectly placed on the edge of the water. The children spilled everywhere, starting a game of primitive rounders, while John and I set about lighting a barbecue. We eventually succeeded, before I was dragooned into the rounders match that was being played without any rules. I found running very difficult with the three Dinnis girls attached to my leg, given that I was already feeling a little weary after having done all the paddling in our canoe.

I checked on Julie and Gundrada. They had been chatting together and were now sitting with their feet up, reading. This looked like the restful idyll I had promised. I felt quite chipper. I sashayed a little closer, offering a glass of wine and uttering the slightly hopeful question "Is everything alright?"

The campsite was great, the children were happy, the weather perfect and the river sumptuous, they both agreed. Clearly, from this answer, I felt something must be wrong. A husband's instincts are tempered in the heat of eternal duty, so I knew something was up. Naturally, I was right.

"We can't find the hot showers," said Julie. She had a sweetly direct manner.

"Are we going to subsist entirely on bread and sausages?" asked Gundrada, not altogether unfairly given the morning's panic buying episode in Hereford when John and I had discovered that the holiday was not a catered adventure. He was currently engrossed in the blackening of an enormous number of sausages on the barbecue. He was too sensible to get involved in my ability to keep digging until I couldn't escape, and carefully kept his back to our little group. I knew he was listening, but, equally, I knew that I was on my own on this one.

There was a fourth tent that had a pole strung across the roof. It had a large bucket with holes in it next to the entrance. The shower was operated by filling the bucket with water heated on the fire, then hanging the bucket over head. I thought that even an estate agent could not really describe that as a hot shower. The plastic porta-loos were both blocked, but, fortunately, located away from our wigwams. Ablution of any description looked, at best, primitive.

"I think you promised us hot showers," said Gundrada matter-of-factly, as if addressing a child who was rather hopeless but of whom she was rather fond. Yet, our setting was so lovely that this was as far as the problematical enquiry went. I think that what Gundrada was really saying was "Well done for getting us all here to enjoy this halcyon day." I joined John for a quick swim in the river. We feasted on bread and sausages before retreating to our respective wigwams, John and I to sleep, wives to read and children for an all night card game.

In the middle of the night, Gundrada entered our tent, waking both of us. "Please can I have another mattress, my futon is a Japanese instrument of torture." Sleepily we located a spare one and she went back out into the night. I went straight back to sleep, mainly because I had already bagged the other spare mattress to compensate for the extraordinary discomfort of my own futon. Peace was not to reign long. Julie appeared in the door and asked John if there was another spare mattress. I was sleeping on it, so pretended to still be asleep.

"Hole's got it, wake him up," John suggested. But I was already awake and, with an admirable pretence at gallantry, handed over the spare bedding. The remainder of my night was spent trying to get comfortable and I eventually dispensed with the futon altogether. Despite my exhausting day, I slept little.

The following morning was another fantastic sunny one and John and I were up early lighting the fire on which we cooked breakfast, which included blackened sausages, a mound of bacon and a few eggs. As the children began to appear, a pattern of activity manifested itself inside my tired mind. In fact, with the nocturnal disturbances, caused entirely by the adults, and the discomfort of the futons, I had not slept properly for two nights. I handle tiredness very badly and have always maintained that were I a prisoner of war, one sleepless night would just about be enough for me to reveal any secrets to a sadistic interrogator. Two sleepless nights had caused me to slip into a realm of feverish imaginings.

The pattern of activity that I hallucinated was of young James, who is older than young George, seeming to follow Florence everywhere she went. Now Florence is tall, blonde and blue-eyed, and like her sister Poppy, has the looks of a super model. Her ethereal nature, though, is in contrast to Poppy's tom boy practicality and clearly had caught the teenaged-boy's imagination.

"I think James fancies Florence," I said to John, forlornly, as we shovelled the piles of bacon round the giant frying pan.

"Can't blame him for that," said John, unhelpfully, and then with some merriment, "you are going to have to deal with this sort of thing sooner or later, you know."

But my mind was both febrile and slugged with sleeplessness. I felt a rather defensive irritation. James, who I had liked before this, was a good sort of boy, loving the canoeing and being really helpful around the campsites. I knew I could not discuss my suspicions with Gundrada, her attitude to this sort of thing was that it was totally natural. She would find my grouchy irrationality amusing.

In this exhausted and melancholic frame of mind I finished breakfast and got ready for the day's journey. I opted to get at least one of the twins into my boat in the hope of getting a little help with the days paddling. Being especially dull of wit, I managed to get James, Florence and Issie in my boat. Issie began singing her song about being a "little teapot." I clenched my teeth.

Once on the Wye again, the sun and the water and the gorgeous landscape through which we passed lifted my spirits. My worries about Gundrada not getting her luxury-tent pampering and the recently suspected serpent of teenaged yearnings were left on the bank. The river transported me, once again, into the gentle bosom of another halcyon day.

The Wye has many moods. The glory of summer was the mood we were enjoying, but the river edges bore the scarring of other, more violent activity. Rising in mountains with high rainfall, the Wye could flood dramatically and the river, in those conditions, could transport large boulders and rip trees from the banks as it churned its silt-laden waters destructively down the great valley. The river level could be two or three metres above the gentle glimmering of water on which we currently floated.

On a wide bend we could see a cloud of sand martins, which were tending young in a colony marked by hundreds of tiny holes in the face of a muddy cliff, perhaps three metres high. The chatter of the birds and their individual acrobatics within the fecund hyper-activity of the swarm was a marvellous event to behold. All the canoes stopped to enjoy this spectacle. There were birds carrying insects into the holes, birds catching insects and still other dipping elegantly into the water to drink. The drama of the great martin colony was so beautifully enhanced by the brilliance of the many acts of aerial gymnastics. I was pleased to see that all crews were soaking up this dramatic display.

I confess to once having Googled my own name, Martin Hole, and had been presented with the world of sand martin holes. The information was much more interesting than that which I had been seeking. The little birds quarry tunnels up to four feet in length, with a narrow entrance of only a couple of inches. In subsequent years, when the birds return from their winter quarters, such excavation is replaced by spring cleaning to get rid of old nest material and any parasite infestations. They can raise two broods, sometimes of as many as five each, before returning to Africa in the autumn. The cliff location should be secure from predators, but the omnivorous badger is known, on the banks of The Wye, to dig down over a meter from above, in order to eat the eggs, or, even tastier, the nestlings. It is one of many creatures that succeed in predating these bountiful colonies.

At Montague and all along the south coast of England, these birds gather both when they arrive in the spring and in even greater numbers when they leave in the autumn. We see clouds of swallows, martins and swifts in these autumn gatherings, in their thousands, weighing down telephone lines or swarming around the feet of the livestock when we are moving mobs of sheep or cattle around the marshes. They are a great pleasure, but a food source for the most agile of birds of prey, the hobby, which is lethally capable of catching them on the wing, and which we also see at home. It is an avian equivalent of the leopards of the Serengetti preying on the antelopes of the The Great Migration.

We had lunch on a river bank beneath a Victorian suspension bridge, in a field inhabited by a herd of pure-bred Hereford cattle. The deep bronze of their coats gleamed healthily in the sun, and John and I advanced towards them, used to the companionable nature of our own cattle. These natives, however, took one look at the two farmers, clad in their orange and red cagoules, and ran for the hills.

The afternoon of our halcyon day sped past with the glory of the riverine summer turned on to full beam. I thought back to my shattered nervous condition of the morning and reflected on how the river had eased away the tension, purifying me of fretfulness and replenishing my energy. I could even talk to young James, whose attachment to Florence now seemed perfectly within the bounds of youthful friendship.

That evening the camp-site was in a remote patch of bank-side scrub. We had it just to ourselves once again. Gundrada and Julie seemed very relaxed. No mention was made of the futon, nor the bucket that doubled as the hot shower. They even took over the cooking duties, although that may have been an act of self-preservation.

I wandered off with John and fairly soon we were lost. As this was merely the natural habitat for John, it did not matter greatly. To re-enforce our meditative detachment a barn owl appeared, hunting diaphanously over the rough grassland for voles to take back to its family. Its ghostly presence in the softening summer gloaming was a vision of great affirmation. The river had cleansed and re-vitalised us. The wise owl was making sure that we knew.

On the last day we were collected from the river, just below the township of Ross, and taken back to Camp One at the farm of our host. John and I ambled off again and were found inspecting the extensive cider apple orchards by the elderly, but energetic, father of the host farmer. When he discovered that John and I were also farmers (and not trespassers), he took us for a tour of the family enterprises in an extremely old Lada. He showed us the orchards, other crops and his son's cattle. He also took us through the village to show off various little property developments. He was an enterprising character. The temperature gauge showed red in the dashboard of the clapped out Lada so he drove us to his home, where he had a second Lada even older than the one in which we were travelling. He simply swapped cars and we carried on with the farm tour.

We bid farewell to the Dinnissiae and en route home to Sussex we stopped at Tewkesbury Abbey. It sits on the confluence of The Avon and The Severn, and in recent years has regularly appeared on the news, photographed from a helicopter during floods, standing above the waters with quiet resolution. The Saxon founders of the Abbey were the Dukes of Mercia, Oddo and Doddo, a fact my children refused to believe. However, the story I most enjoyed about the Abbey was not the names of its founders, nor the massacre that took place there during the War of the Roses, but the fact that the people of Tewkesbury had banded together in 1541 to defy Henry VIII, saving the beautiful building with its impressive square Norman tower from his programme of church destruction. They purchased the building from the Crown for £453. I do enjoy hearing of local communities defying authority to achieve the conservation of that which is special in their own environments.

On exiting the Abbey, I purchased a long sought after recording of Rutter's Requiem. When we resumed the journey home I offered the family the choice of Rutter and his hauntingly melodic mass, or Test Match Special. Although caught on the horns of a dilemma, so much had they all enjoyed the Wye that they tolerated my departure into self-indulgence and I happily flitted between the two on the journey home.

Chapter 6

The Wye - Absolutely frozen - January 2013
By Will Miller,
a bit by Martin
and a bit by Dick Forrest

Before I hand the narrative over to my friend Will, I will endeavour to set the scene. The summer holiday on the Wye had been a marked success, but the journey had been terminated at Ross-on Wye. The stretch of river from Ross down to Monmouth takes in the hills and stunning cliffs of Symonds Yat, a mini-mountain home to peregrine falcons and ravens, and the river becomes more exciting, with several rapids to descend. In the summer, while I had visited Tewkesbury, John had taken his family to explore the Yat. He was as keen as mustard to return, as was I. Thus it became our choice of January excursion.

Will lived next door to Montague. He had arrived in the village after marrying one of the prettiest girls in the county, the lovely Audrey. He is a properly mad Australian, with a doctorate in English Literature, and is passionate about the Irish writer James Joyce. To most of us James Joyce's writings represent the addled ramblings of a superbly incoherent Irish ne'er do well. To Will it was the very soul of humanity that was revealed.

I had always thought that James Joyce was a one-off, one of those singular Irish literary geniae, but I had recently been on a cricket tour to Dublin, where I had played for a team called The Leprechauns. A farming friend had sent me their annual cricket report, which was written in the same bizarre absurd semi consciousness as *Ulysses*, Joyce's great novel. I will provide an excerpt from this surprise work of literary genius; (by Dick Forrest, not James Joyce!)

"Mid-June meant the "jollye olde" Sussex Farmers were on their bi-annual Dublin visit. Sadly their trip was marred by the *shameless* bumping of their usual Trinity match, this to facilitate a semi-professional *franchise* making the college Park their home.

Polite enquiries were met with an offer of....wait for it...*Bird Avenue* (but you'd have to find your own opposition!!). More (much) in a mo.. Just as happened when nets couldn't be found for a visiting Canadian team, the Leps were on the case. Michael Brown provided Phoenix in the Great Park (and two lovely bar maids!). Let the fun commence...

At Castle ave, the previous day (or more likely in Rangan's bar earlier (very) that morning), the Farmers persuaded Zander, Boer not Fish, to switch sides (I hasten to add NOT in the biblical sense). They shopped well. He took 5/32 in our 240 all out. Castleknock out half, Adam Chester, got a masterful ton... and Zanders "swapee" Martin Hole (class, class, put your bibles away!!) a paltry hungover 5. As play got going, one of the Farmers approached the bar....Barmaid (callow, red haired pretty) "Would you like a pint, Sir?"

"Well, No actually, I'm looking for *eighteen*!!!"

She sighed, semi-orgasmically, "I'll get a tray, Sir."

Five hot hours (and a fresh barrel of Guinness) later all 4 results were on. Farmers 234/9 in the penultimate over, Zander at the non-strikers end and Hole due to bowl the last. The out half sealed the deal by bowling Brierly, the farmers No.11. Hole stayed up the sleeve. Barrel No.3 was soon tapped...."

Will's grasp of Joyce is professorial, though when confronted by Dick's Leprechaun Match Report, he confessed that Joyce was the easier to comprehend. My understanding of Joyce is such that Dick should really take this as a compliment.

We discovered the Wye in January to be a very different animal to that which we had enjoyed in the summer. Its mood now was brutal. Leaden, cold-grey currents slid in freezing cohorts down its length. A far greater volume of water than on our summer visit flowed between the now joyless banks.

If you understood The Leprechaun's cricket report, then read on with pleasure. If not, then scratch your head like the rest of us! Good Luck, and Over to Will!

"It was explained to me that I should be prepared for character assassination in later chapters, but to get my blow in first, I readily accepted the invitation to report on the above mentioned canoe trip. My cunning plan is to undermine the veracity of witnesses to any events I was party to in later chapters, and to polish my own standing in the eyes of the reader, to the point that no far-fetched, bizarre story involving men in wetsuits would ever be accepted unconditionally. Except for that town mayor in the middle of Normandy giving us all a French bollocking as we tiptoed across his bulbs, canoes on shoulders. All the rest – bah!

However, I have to confess to not remembering very much about this trip, due to cognitive impairment, which I put down entirely to having given up drinking alcohol. I am told I drank some seventeen pints the night before the canoe trip itself, which should not overly affect a chap, if indeed at all, but, because I had given up drinking, it had the most deleterious effect. That said, the witnesses who provided me with this suspiciously precise number of pints are the very same witnesses I have forewarned the reader about, and so any information provided is highly suspect. I have taken it upon myself here to sift fact from fiction and again insist that anything written after this chapter must be considered as mere myth or, possibly, legend.

Any canoe trip really begins weeks before with preparation. As a non-farming invitee I bore no responsibility for logistics or accommodation and ducked much of the serious flack that inevitably follows such duties. I quickly came to appreciate that the quality of the digs, and availability of appropriate cuisine on such adventures can attract exponentially adverse ridicule. My duties were more circumscribed: a teenage surfer almost half a century ago, my old wet suit decomposed much like a pharaoh's face when a sarcophagus is opened, and new attire had to be sourced. Surfing the net, I was rather surprised that so many other people also indulge in canoeing, although, if typically it is classed an insanity of sorts, I suspect Martin and John's might well be the full delusional, psychopathic sort. Of course, that is not how these canoeing adventures were first introduced to me.

One custom I was prepared for was to be able to talk at some length about a particular area of expertise, and that for me was straightforward – fencing (specifically "sword fighting," for my farming readers). Martin, having exhausted several encyclopaedias of knowledge on previous trips was scratching for something to say. Given his various awards for making swamps and, possibly because we had barely five minutes before departure, he was grateful for my suggestion of reciting Gerald Manley Hopkin's poem 'The Windhover,' about a falcon, and printed out a copy for himself.

> I caught this morning morning's minion,
>
> Kingdom of daylight's dauphin, dapple-dawn-drawn Falcon, in his riding
>
> Of the rolling level underneath him steady air, and striding

Reciting it at the Ross Royal Hotel, full of local revellers, would have chimed so well with the lovely peregrines who nest in the cliffs of nearby Yat Rock. The room would have quietened to hear the Anglo-Saxon alliteration, the clever rhymes, intoned by a Citizen with oaken forearms and legs (and surely it is gorse he has growing over them), a man-mountain who, with pint in hand, could have been mistaken for a giant resurrected from the steep, green valley sides. Such was not to be, however, despite my vigorous prompting at various carefully selected moments that evening, generally whenever a goodly audience was present.

> High there, how he rung upon the rein of a wimpling wing
>
> In his ecstasy! then off, off forth on swing,
>
> As a skate's heel sweeps smooth on a bow-bend: the hurl and gliding

Rebuffed the big wind. My heart in hiding

Stirred for a bird,—the achieve of, the mastery of the thing!

As it turned out, I was the only participant to have prepared a speech and, when called upon, with dinner plates tidied away and guests relaxing in the bar, I manfully took my place at the podium. Fortunately for my talk the cutlery tray was nearby, and I was able to arm my audience with knives with which to practice the thrust and lunge, compound attacks, feints, disengages, parries of quarte, sixte and octave, various *prises de fer* and ceding parries. Finally, I demonstrated the fleche, which in French means "arrow." The movement involves a running leap, drawn weapon at the fore, plunging it in the arm, chest or head of an opponent. It should be, and was on this occasion, accompanied by a bloodcurdling howl of murderous intent and a ballestra, a savage stamp of the front foot. The hotel management were on the point of telephoning various town officials to intervene, if I hadn't quickly put down the piece of cutlery and retaken my seat as if nothing had happened.

Nonetheless, I believe there was much wringing of hands among the other guests when my talk concluded, and not entirely due to the various pokes and bruises sustained. The other guests looked to my companions-at-paddles, but found them sadly lacking in after dinner entertainment. There was some sort conference on Sewage Treatment in the same hotel and it was inevitable, after possibly the twelfth pint, that we should become exceedingly good friends with quite a few people whom we would never see again. Some of our new friends felt that they too had particular areas of expertise that could be imparted, particularly as the Viking warrior god Woden,(or was it Finn MacCool himself of Irish legend, or even the mighty Achilles of Trojan fame?) found himself too tongue-tied to read out a short poem despite my ever more insistent entreaties. Instead, a Captain of the Sewage Industry stepped into the breach to face the barrage of farmer cannon fire. The Captain explained how he just completed drilling a thirty-kilometre tunnel under the Thames, with a diameter roughly the size of football field. On further questioning, its purpose became clear: to fill it with human excrement. The tunnel had various levels and pumps, and the solidified slurry would, at the other end, squeeze out like toothpaste from an immense tube. Huge trucks mounted with plastic bristles would each take a portion of this amalgam and drive - somewhere. Unfortunately it was around this time that I was overcome with serious cognitive impairment. I later recall awakening to a loud banging on my door, which I first thought might be a marauder and, arming myself with a butter knife, was prepared to stand my ground, only to be informed that it was time to make a seven-hour canoe trip. Martin stood eagerly in the doorway, urging me to hurry or face the forecast blizzards while still on the swollen river.

But I have gotten far ahead of myself. En route to Ross with a modified sheep trailer carrying two canoes, I was introduced to John as The Human Seal. "Just call him The Seal," Martin had said. "He'll understand."

"You must be The Seal," I said, shaking John's damp, webbed paw.

"The what?" he asked, genuinely puzzled.

"I have no idea," I said, still shaking his hand. I looked to Martin, who was suddenly examining something in the glove-box

Conversation continued to be slow after Martin bought an Alicia Key's CD in a petrol station, not the one with "New York" on it, but some later anodyne offering suitable, if played very faintly, for a dentist's waiting room or an elevator. But the *craic* flowed after the discussion swung to EU farmer subsidies, solar power rebates, phosphate levels in wood ash, crop rotation, and multi-fuel energy sources. Various tractors pulling complex agricultural machinery in fields alongside the M3 were spotted and discussed in some obscure farmer's version of I-spy, awarding points, I believe, for specific models and colours.

We picked up George, the fourth member of our canoeing venture. He was also a farmer, but smaller in stature and much neater than Martin and John. I discovered all of them were former members of the Hogwarts School of Agriculture, or some such bizarre institution which has taught for a millennium at least, sacred corn fertility rites to English farmers. These rituals were usually enacted in celebrations held after Old Boy cricket tours, usually involving beer in deeply rural locations. Fate would have it that this college too was in the remote Wye Valley, precisely where we were heading. Canoes in tow, needless to say, I kept watch for banjos – anywhere. (Editor's note - Australian geography clearly at fault here, as the College is in Wye, Kent.)

I felt more at ease later when assigned the title of Honorary Farmer, on the basis that I had a few chickens and ducks. George was waiting for us at yet another farmer's home, a man whom neither Martin nor John knew, although he provided cups of tea and tools for bodging the trailer lights back into action. Martin borrowed a hammer and a spool of cellotape then, looking puzzled, told George to fix the trailer lights. I hadn't seen such goodwill and generosity for unknown travellers since making my way across the Sahara in the 80s, since which time my estimation of human character has dwindled considerably. It spoke volumes for the farming community. Fortunately, I didn't say this out loud.

The sat nav directed us to Ross-on-Wye. The Land Rover and trailer loaded with canoes zigzagged down a steep hill and onwards along a lane that really could only handle a medieval hand cart. After a while it was clear we were on the wrong road. Martin's belief in technology was touching, though mis-guided. He eventually managed a difficult and long reverse back up the tiny single-track lane. One must always allow for several hours of painful delay in any trip.

This dreadful morning after the night before was possibly one of the more miserable experiences one can endure, short of stumbling barefoot to the South Pole. I was very hung over. We changed into wetsuits in a public car park, then put on fleeces and wet weather gear. The temperature was eight degrees below zero. With a snow blizzard predicted, and the river in flood, we faced hour after hour of slow paddling. The three farmers all looked excited and annoyingly well. Surely they had drunk the same amount as I had? We formed pairs and got into the two canoes. Paddle techniques harmonised and conversations spluttered against the mind-numbing cold. Each pairing resembled a pensioner couple. Joint injuries, lumbar ache, muscle fatigue and brain pain, in one big powerful mixture of agony. Someone saw a kingfisher. The peregrines must have all died. Cows had long fled the flooded fields.

There were some moments of true beauty as the river wound through tight turns under steep wooded valley sides. We stopped and went exploring at one point, where a vast gas pumping project had intruded like a deserted ore mine into the quiet of the flood plain. Wet-suited and staggering about in the scree, we were like some larger aquatic beast emergent from the primordial slime. Abandoned stone buildings, plus a few preserved by wealthy professionals as weekend retreats, littered the passing valley floor. Amongst the green fields and riverbank trees, farms wounded by twentieth century economics were showing their scars. A distant egret was disturbed from its hungry scavenging by our approach on the river. A forest or two lurked in the more inaccessible valleys and on higher hilltops, but man had cut and harrowed several forlorn stretches along the banks. It often seemed a defaced national treasure we were passing.

Then there was lunch at a pretty pub, overlooking the much-talked-of rapids at Symonds Yat, with a warming of manky, bluish feet and frozen digits by the wood fire. This was followed by the last leg of the day's journey down to Monmouth. There were supposed to be some rapids along here somewhere, and Martin had been fretting about them, but with the river swollen we passed briskly but harmlessly over the top of them. The large boulders and specially-crafted obstructions were deep below the current river level, so it was nothing to write home about, except perhaps for the fact that John had somehow managed to annoy a convoy of emergency service types, who were crossing the said 'rapids' at this point. They were firemen doing emergency rescue exercises in the freezing fast-flowing water. We departed the scene briskly.

We reached the boat club at Monmouth after a freezing but rapid descent of the river, the clouds deepening to a rich stormy black. The taxi driver eventually arrived, cheerfully stating that he was glad to see us "as only a nutter would do the river in January in this weather." Strapping both our canoes onto its roof, we gratefully climbed into its warm interior and it returned us to Martin's urban assault vehicle and modified sheep trailer. Freed from the death-grip of my wetsuit at last, my entire body felt as clammy and waterlogged as the insides of an oyster.

The promised snow was late to arrive. When it hit we were already homeward bound, the motorway closing down behind us, the wipers clearing the flurry from the windscreen as we flew eastward. Fortunate to make it home that night, we watched the weather over the next few days, blanketing The Wye Valley and the whole of Wales, shutting it down completely.

These are the facts of the matter, as far as I can separate them from the various alternative accounts I have been presented with by witnesses, none of which bear repeating here. For the record, however, I wish to strenuously assert that there was no poker game and I still own my house."

We had greatly enjoyed having Will on our adventure and, on the journey home, conversation once again turned to farming. John knew that Will was a great literary man and thought that because he was a lover of Joyce's writings, he would also be enthusiastic about Heller and *Catch 22*. Will said that the book was "up there with *Finnegans Wake*." The three farmers assumed this was a very high compliment, but we were not entirely certain.

George quietly suggested that James Joyce might have written the agricultural policy behind something called the Soil Protection Review, when he was plastered one day, whereby the ministry deemed that a farm's soil was properly cared for so long as the forms were correctly filled. Will countered by suggesting it was more Sartre, exhibiting a sort of existential detachment between consciousness and reality. Before I could come up with any response to this, which could have been a very long period of time, John licked his lips with relish and said that he had a perfect agricultural Catch 22. To receive subsidies, farmers currently have to conserve all the natural habitats on their land. The amalgamated area of these hedges, woods, ponds and other features is then called a PIF, (permanently ineligible feature). The PIF area is then deducted from the subsidy payment area because the land is deemed to be not in "Good Agricultural Condition." "The larger the habitats, the bigger the deduction that is made from the farm payment. Pure Heller!" said John.

Will laughed sympathetically at our policy predicaments as well as our literary ignorance. He felt that in the activity of our canoeing we were all more Joyce than Heller. He had enjoyed the addled ramblings of three incoherent English ne'er do wells for the last couple of days. Never before had a journey home from one of our adventures achieved such intellectual heights. Thank you Will.

Chapter 7
The Canche, Normandy, France - April 2013

As recalled by John

"Paddle, you fool!" I urged my canoe partner. It was dawn and we were stuck against the central pier of a gorgeous, arched stone bridge, on the verge of being swamped by the fast flowing water of the Canche. We were behind a church and surrounded by quaint medieval buildings in the centre of the little Normandy town of Hesdin. Martin just giggled, rocking with mirth when he should have been steering.

The Canche was my choice. While studying a map looking for suitable rivers to attack in April I was struck by the fact that France was closer to our homes than the West Country. The Channel was a small obstacle, though "Manche" (the French name for The Channel) rhymed with "Canche" and I could foresee a deviation into nonsense verse on the horizon. It was not many millennia ago that The Thames and the Rhine shared the same estuary and the mantle of chalk covering the south east of England also covered the north of France in one continuous sheet. Plate tectonics, ice ages and dam-busting seas may have conspired to divorce us from the continent and to still be widening The Channel, but they were not going to deter us from mounting a canoe expedition to the lovely chalk stream that is the Canche. An hour's drive from Calais, this charming little river rises on the chalk of Haut Normandy and tumbles prettily to the sea at a mighty estuary with miles of salt marshes, north of the fashionable coastal resort of Le Touquet.

Martin was initially a bit chary about my plan, but quickly became cheery when he realised what a great river we were to visit. He lambs until mid-April and is totally exhausted at this time of year, so when speaking to him makes very little sense. A quick paddle is thus hugely restorative to both of us as, contrary to his assertion that all arable farmers are idle, I too have a busy Spring on the farm.

On our journey to catch the Dover car ferry we organised to leave my car with our old Rustic friend, Nigel, who lives not far from the ferry terminal. He is one of the senior statesmen of the Tour, and part of the gang of elders that the youngsters refer to as The Woolly Mammoths. Of that group, he is the closest of us to fit that description.

We arrived at his home, an immaculate farmhouse set in well tended gardens, to have breakfast with his son Toby. Nigel, being an idle arable farmer, was away walking in the Atlas Mountains.... We had invited him to come canoeing with us, but his excuse was that he was too busy. Too busy walking, it turns out, to be doing any canoeing or any work. Our first opportunity for mischief presented itself. Nigel's garden, when we arrived, was being mown by two robotic lawn mowers. After he had first acquired them, one had driven itself into the swimming pool and the other into the flower border. Nigel claimed that he now had them completely under control. Martin and I removed the lid from the well, in the hope that one of these automatons would find its way into its watery depths. Unfortunately we were caught by Toby, who could hear the pair of us laughing stupidly above the noise of the sizzling bacon. He did not want to be blamed for the demise of his Dad's latest toy. Our plot was foiled.

Nigel has been a very entrepreneurial farmer. He managed to lose a lot of money farming worms, but has made it back in spades (sorry) on houses in Chelsea, and latterly on wind farms. He wears bright red trousers that match his complexion and once arrived on a Rustics tour wearing a Panama hat. There is no record, of course, of him ever leaving the Rustics with "that" hat, though there is recollection of an incident in which a hat fitting the description was shot with a twelve-bore on the lawn of Horn Park during a mole hunt. Charming and genial, Nige is always full of interesting conversation. This is just as well for, like myself and Martin, his batting duties had been reduced to a minimum, and during a cricket match he had much time on his hands to revel in this art. As a batsman he was known for a chopping "slap" of the ball rather hard through the covers. In the field, he resembled a tall piece of unsteady antique furniture, eliciting creaking noises from all other Rustics if he ever managed to bend over enough to stop the ball.

He has the gift of being able to laugh at himself. This landed him in trouble with the Rustic Fines Committee a few years ago when he let on that he had inadvertently rented out a farm cottage to a middle-aged hooker. He was amused to find his farming empire supported in this way by "the oldest profession." After some debate about what actually is the "oldest profession," he was duly fined for "living off the earnings of a high class Lady."

We thanked Toby for a fine breakfast, and set off in Martin's Skoda with the canoe on its roof, ratchet straps singing happily in the wind. The queue for the ferry was made interesting by the car behind. Martin was wittering excitedly about a "boat on a car on a boat," but behind us was an "aeroplane on a car on a boat." As usual, the gregarious farmer was soon in deep conversation with these fellow passengers. The plane had been made in Norfolk, folded into a size smaller than a car, and was being delivered to a customer in Germany. It had a new safety feature, an exploding parachute mechanism, which would deploy in a mid-air crisis. I explained to the plane men that we had seen this technology before, in an exploding life jacket, used by one of our canoeing guests on the river Taw. They greatly enjoyed the story of Simon emerging from the water like some NASA space rocket leaving earth.

We arrived in France in warm spring sunshine and headed south towards Etaples, stopping in a seaside resort on the way for a very civilized lunch. We reached Etaples in late afternoon, and took the road that followed the river inland. Our first view of the river was of a gracefully gentle, meandering water way. Willows bowed to the water's edge, in a scene of rural harmony that could have been painted by Constable, had he been a Frenchman. Further along we left the river bank and drove up onto the chalk hills above the river valley. Little lanes and small fields with small numbers of cattle gave way to an area of high farming. Large granaries could be seen in modern farmyards, and tractors were busy planting potatoes in very large fields. The freshly cultivated ground revealed a deep loam, superb arable soil, far removed from the thin, flinty soils we have at home. Even Martin, who professed to know very little about technical arable farming, expressed an admiration for the farms we were driving past.

I had devised a plan for the Canche, elegant in its simplicity. A railway ran along the river valley, so we could canoe from the river source to the sea and easily return to the Skoda left at our launch point. This was a far simpler plan than those usually insisted upon by Martin. I thought it important to make that point clear to him.

"Something will muck it up," he retorted, with great assurance.

For the first night we were booked into a little hotel bar called the Hotel La Chope, on the outskirts of the pretty town of Hesdin. Our host was an English man called Eric who, after Martin had stopped speaking in French, took a great interest in our proposed trip. I explained that we would take two days to get from the top of The Canche to the sea and that, after the first day's paddling, we would stay at The Hotel de France in the ancient Napoleonic castle of Montreuil-sur-mer. (He thought that to be a superb place to stop). The second day we would canoe as far as the great estuary, to the fishing port of Etaples, then catch a train back to Hesdin to collect our car. He was impressed by our ambition, even calling it intrepid, but immediately explained that the return journey would be impossible because the train line we needed was currently closed for engineering repairs.

I dared not look at Martin, but noticed in the mirror behind the bar that the farmer had removed his six foot four inch frame from the stool and was performing a cross between an Irish jig and a South Sea Island war dance on the floor of the saloon. Grinning like the Cheshire cat, he did not need to use the phrase "told you so." His dance was more eloquent. Eric looked a little concerned, but quickly realised his guests were enjoying a moment of oddly English humour. He relaxed and, after another beer, he suggested a solution to the collapse of my elegant plan. He offered to drive the Skoda down to Etaples to collect us, as he wanted very much to hear the outcome of our proposed adventure. Another English couple arrived at the bar from whom we learned of a large ex-pat population living and holidaying in the area. The region is called the Sept Valees, and Eric was a resident Mr Fix-it for this community, looking after their property affairs. The evening was rounded off nicely at a local restaurant in the town centre.

Both sets of our children had recently started referring to our canoe trips as Brokeback Tours, after the film about the malicious persecution of gay cowboys. Earlier in the year, during a school holiday outing, I had been at an Indian curry house in Hastings with the triplets, Rosie, Issie and Hattie. Two men had come into the restaurant and Rosie had looked enquiringly at them and then asked me, in a whisper fortunately, whether they were gay. I cautiously explained that it was quite normal for two men to eat together, and they were "probably just friends."

"Hole and I eat together all the time on canoeing trips," I said, trying to allay this slightly awkward, childish line of curiosity, "and no one would raise an eyebrow at that."

Hattie took a sharp intake of breath. "But he is the gayest-looking man I know," she iterated with all the worldliness a twelve year old girl from the country could muster. Little did I know that this conversation would come back to haunt us on the Canche.

Relevant to our story also, Hastings was the birth-place of Archibald Belaney, who became famous from living with the Ojibwe Indians in the early 20th century. Under the pseudonym of Grey Owl, his graphic writings and passionate advocacy made him one of the "most effective apostles of the wilderness." He particularly espoused the cause of the beaver, which hitherto had been heavily trapped, as well as championing the wider issues of nature conservation. Pictures of him canoeing in lakes dressed as an Indian caught the public imagination. His popularity later diminished when it was revealed that the exotic Grey Owl was actually Hastings born and bred. Despite the prescience and inspiration of his message he was shunned and died of chronic alcoholism aged just 49. The canoe we used on our adventures aptly bore the name Ojibwe, so I felt a connection to this enigmatic son of Sussex.

Anyway, I digress, so let's return to the Canche itself. It is dawn and Martin and I are still arguing, in a way that has become a ritual, about the best launch point. Should we get in further up-stream, or go for a little slipway that entered the river by the restaurant we had visited last night. The slipway was in the town centre next to a church and crowded in by the narrow streets of the old part of town. We went with the slipway and carried the canoe through the town centre to the recently negotiated launch point. Whilst it was early in the morning, Hesdin was like a ghost-town. We had noted a certain state of desertion about the place the night before. There was no rush hour at all, so portage of a canoe through the town centre was extremely easy.

The river is tightly funnelled as it passes through the built area of the town. River banks are the walls and footings of the houses. The current was unexpectedly brisk, a fact that Eric had warned us of the night before. The first hundred yards after launch had been like a scene from the set of an adventure movie, so fast were we moving. Martin, despite his battered hat, was no Indiana Jones however, and that was how our present predicament, wedged to the central pier of the bridge, came about.

We did manage to remove ourselves without further mishap and without a drenching. It was a happy start to what would be a long day of paddling and we continued through the town, the sunrise catching the water briefly and lighting the buildings beautifully. Soon the countryside reappeared and the raison d'etre for The Canche journey was laid plain. We were in a foreign country in a gorgeous setting, no phones, no cars, no duties and no cares but for the navigation of the river.

The Canche is one of a clutch of chalk rivers that rise in Normandy and flow to the coast. Chalk rivers are unique to this part of the globe, either side of the Channel, and have the benefit of being fed from a landscape that filters the water before releasing it slowly into the streams. The chemical infusion gives us "soft" water, but its purity gives it a translucence and health in which fish, plants and insects abound. They are special places, adorned by the convexo-concavity of the chalk slopes, and in France, as in England, are highly protected. We have one such river, the Darent, running through the farm. We have protected pastures and trees along its course to encourage the wildlife, the cleanness of the water and augment its pretty landscaped setting. The farmers along The Canche were managing the riverbanks to achieve the same objectives. Martin said to look out for floating tresses of river water crowfoot and that we should get to see water voles. Canoeing in April opened many opportunities not to be had in January, the flora being one such pleasure. We were quickly discovering that canoeing in summer conditions without the terror of falling into freezing or flood level water, was wonderfully relaxing.

The Canche did not differ from many other chalk rivers in the number of mills that it once supported. Now virtually all of them are either deserted ruins, or converted to other uses. In their heyday the industry and employment along the river must have been considerable, and all powered by the perpetual energy of the river. We passed mills about every mile or two, and several provided us with amusing features to get the canoe through. Broken weirs and cluttered mill channels came along regularly, which provided entertainments in the predominately swift-flowing but gentle current. Several of the old mills were giant affairs and we stopped to explore a few of these forgotten relics, poking about in large crumbled old wheel houses, marvelling at the size of the stone block work and the extent of the river engineering. We were wrapt by the ludicrous quirk of history that had rendered this industry, based wholly on a source of free power and cheap transportation, redundant.

The morning had flown towards lunch. We decided to stop at a very pretty village where old apple trees were in blossom and brown dairy cows watched us from their small fields. A bucolic haze of warmth suffused our own little world. We pulled out of the water near a grand old farmhouse with attached cattle yards. It felt French in a timeless way. We hid the canoe in some brambles and ambled to a bar and then, because lunch was not to be found there, to a patisserie in which a very pretty girl was in the process of shutting up the shop. We executed our best "franglais" to encourage her to prepare a jambon sandwich, which she declined, but we left her sparkling shop with a box of large and rather filling cream cakes. She had flirted in a sweetly teasing manner with both of us, though Martin reckoned, wrongly of course, that it was mainly with him. We left the little village wholly enamoured, with her and with life generally.

To get to Montreuil we still had quite a long way to go. The water remained brisk and we made good time, but we did have to keep paddling. Increasingly along the river banks we were hearing strange splashing and seeing fleeting glimpses of brown furry river mammals. This was not the gentle activity, as described by Martin, when telling me the habits of the water vole. Where were the carefully constructed little tunnels along the water's edge, and why was there no sign of the carefully laid out vole hamlets with little paths, food stores and latrines that he had claimed were so distinctive a part of the water voles presence along a river? I asked Martin, but he did not know the answer. No Latin names were forthcoming, just a puzzled reply about the size of the holes being far too big and the animals themselves being much too large. We were both stumped by this creature that we were encountering. It turned out that they were muskrats, a species introduced from North America where their numbers are controlled by predators such as lynx, bears and wolves. Their absence from Florida is attributed entirely to the appetite of the alligators. As such carnivores were not to be found in this part of France, the muskrat population had increased unchecked and was now having a negative impact on the river banks. Locals were trying hard to eradicate this pest using cage traps which they had put out all along the river bank. It looked liked the work of Canute.

We pressed on and as tea time approached amused ourselves with the oft repeated observation that Montreuil would appear round the next bend. When the town did eventually appear, we were very relieved. Our last obstacle then hove into view, an artificially constructed canoe slalom course built by the Montreuil canoe club. Swinging between the poles and the big rocks in the white-water was a great finale to the day, though Martin claimed that I had aimed the canoe directly at the slalom poles so that each of them would whack him on the noodle.

Our progress through the slalom had thus gone something like this:

"Left," would shout Martin, sighting a rock

"Ouch!" He would then utter

"Big rock ahead!"

"Ouch!" then followed again

"Mind the pole!"

"Oooof!"

"Steer Dinnis!"

"OOOaargh!"

I hadn't enjoyed steering a boat as much as this ever before.

Below the rapids were some steps, at which we got ourselves and the canoe out of the water. We were knackered, looking forward to the comforts of the Hotel de France. According to my map it should have been where we were standing, right beside the river...but no building of the sort could be seen. A little exploration yielded the information that the hotel was in the middle of the town on top of the hill. The hill was faced by a cliff and a road wound steeply up to the mighty town walls and through a fortified gate, which was the entrance to the town.

The rampart walls surrounding this town are impressive. In 1544 they had successfully kept out the marauding army of Henry VIII. Several hundred years later the citadel was used as the headquarters for Napoleon, when he was considering the invasion of England. Apart from increased fortification, he left a lasting legacy to three nearby villages, naming them to immortalise stages in his lovemaking to the Empress Josephine. Hence Le Catleyage, La Culbute and Attin la Paix Faite gained their monikers. Long before all this the town was a busy port, with a community of dyers and weavers who turned English wool into cloth and then sold it back to the English. Often dyed green, this cloth is claimed to be the same as that in which Robin Hood and his Merry Men famously dressed. Wool was heavily taxed and the trade in it was often carried out by gangs of smugglers crossing The Channel. Wool left England in exchange for wine and spirits, cloth, lace and tobacco. There are tunnels beneath the farm at Montague, which Martin had shown me, dug by the gangs for stealthily conveying this contraband in defiance of the Customs officers. It may even have been wool produced from the Montague flock which crossed over to the dyers and weavers of Montreuil....

Modern Montreuil, unlike Hesdin, had a proper rush hour which clogged its narrow streets. We had to carry the canoe up the hill, then along the narrow aisles of the ancient citadel through this heavy traffic. Wet suited and hang-dog tired, we eventually made it to the hotel. It looked straight out of *The Three Musketeers* and is one of the oldest buildings in this extraordinary town. The reason I had thought the hotel to be on the water's edge was because the tourist map had failed to show the contours of the cliff on which the town perched. Martin was gleeful yet again.

We entered the hotel courtyard, festooned in colourful hanging baskets filled with spring flowers. The Landlord greeted us rather frostily, but thawed a little when he noticed his guests were wearing wet suits and carrying a canoe. We were pointed to our palatial room which had Persian carpets and authentic tapestry on the walls. It was sumptuous, but it only had one bed. We showered and changed and went back to the hotel bar.

I spoke to the landlord, who was a tall South African, married to the very sparky English owner of the building:

"Er, the room is lovely but it has only got one bed."

"Well, my secretary very definitely said that is what you wanted. That there would be two men and you wanted a double bed. Apparently you were quite adamant."

Martins' face was dissolving and he began to make a strange gulping sound. Tears started to appear on his cheeks. He had worked out exactly what had happened. I had used my best French to order a double room, but it had translated into double bed. The Landlord also seemed to have warmed towards us, possibly relieved not to have to imagine how his gorgeous bedroom was going to be the scene of a night of athletic, male sex. I mentioned my wife and children, just to make sure we were being understood correctly. Our room was duly changed to a double and we had a very enjoyable evening drinking with both our hosts. The hotel felt like home, though we were the only guests, and our landlord treated us as old friends.

The bonhomie was such that in the morning they took a picture of the pair of us sitting in the canoe in their courtyard and put it on the celebrity visitor photo board in the foyer, next to Mel Smith, the famous comedian. That was more apt than they realised. Martin and I often dine together and can be sat at the table for hours, in part because Martin is a painfully slow eater. We are as good a couple of talking heads as you'll ever meet and Mel Smith had an act with Griff Rhys Jones in which their two heads would be silhouetted, talking nonsense to each other. For many years before this journey Martin had been fond of referring to our meals together as Smith and Jones evenings.

The journey from Montreuil to Etaples was shorter than the journey we had taken from Hesdin. We had time for a leisurely breakfast and a tour of the amazing walled town and its Napoleonic brick ramparts before we took the canoe back down the cliff to the river. Martin seemed keen to start where we had left off, but I insisted we had to have another go at the slalom. He steered this time and the journey down the rapid elicited the exact reverse of the conversation we had while descending it the first time. I'm not sure it was such a good idea.

About a mile below Montreuil we passed a car park beside the river. There we watched a man in an immaculately polished Saab motor car unload a state-of-the-art racing kayak and proceed to paddle up river, against the current. He made the strenuous task look effortless. He stopped when he got to our canoe and we greeted one another. Peering over the side of our boat he noticed our boots.

"It is dangerous to wear wellingtons," he said in heavily accented English, before disappearing up the river like a salmon. The image of the travel writer Eric Newby meeting Wilfred Thesiger, a tough and ascetic traveller, on his *Short Walk in the Hindu Kush* sprang to mind, in which Newby's air bed is discovered and scorned by Thesiger. Unlike the great explorer the kayakist stopped short of calling us "a couple of pansies," despite our pathetic paddling with the current and our inappropriate footwear.

The river began to slow and show signs of salt water incursion. The banks bore the marks of the tide. We hadn't factored this into our plans so high up the river. Then I noticed an inn at a little village we were passing through. It was the last chance for lunch before a long haul down the river across open country towards the sea. A fence prevented us from getting from the river to the front door, so we tip-toed through a back yard filled with ducks and chickens, entering the inn through the back door of the kitchen.

Our unorthodox entrance and Martin's best French, which included an elaborate greeting, prompted the Maitre to exclaim that the Marine Royale had arrived. Martin affected insult and insisted we were actually the Royal Navy, coming to finish what Henry VIII had failed to achieve. Fortunately his French was not quite up to history badinage, so our host just looked at him curiously. We were a bit early for food, so he served us several beers before a delicious plate of ham and cheese arrived. He too was intrigued by the nature of our journey.

After lunch we encountered an ordeal by wind. Etaples was not far, but a sea breeze made hard work of the journey through the coastal plain. Paddling was exhausting, but eventually we drew up in the middle of the fishing port at the neck of the great estuary. The ordeal was not quite finished, however, as we had to get ourselves and the boat over the mud flats to the quayside where our hotel was located. We eventually scrambled out of this waist deep black ooze and knocked on the door of our hotel on the far side of the road. The lady on the other side of the glass door pointed at the white curtains and the shiny floor and we gathered that we were not going to be allowed in until we had cleaned ourselves. Fortunately we had clean clothes in our dry bags, and returned to the creeks of the salt marshes to peel off our fetid wet-suits. We changed into normal clothes which sufficed for us to be granted entry.

Eric collected us as arranged, in Martin's Skoda, and over yet another beer in his hotel we told him of our travels. We then hurried back down to Etaples for a delicious fish supper in the famed Fisherman's Co-operative and another evening of Smith and Jones. We sat on our table for two, overlooking the vast estuary in the spring moonlight, re-living the life of the river we had just descended. Our first overseas trip had been a resounding success and we returned to England mentally refreshed but physically spent.

Martin drove me back to Nigel's house to collect my car. No one was at home this time. While transferring my bag from his car we heard a whirring noise coming from the lawn. We looked at each other and, for a moment, exhaustion departed. The robotic mowers were hard at work. The well was unguarded. Well, all is well that ends well!

Chapter 8
The Exe twice in 2013
and some Epic Animal Impersonations

By Martin

The first year when John and I were dropped from the Rustics versus Dumplings match led to trouble. We had found ourselves with little to do, in the city centre of Exeter. A pleasant drink in a wine bar with a pretty hostess, at 11 o'clock in the morning, had given us the information we needed. Three of the younger, trendier, Rustics were wearing some supposedly fashionable, but actually hideous, trousers that revealed their underpants. We had decided, with the blessing of the all powerful Fines Committee, that they should be showing off something a little sexier, if it was knickers that they wished to display. Our hostess at the wine bar told us where we could buy suitable lingerie for the boys. Off we went, purchasing from a lady's boutique a bizarre assortment of garments that we did not really understand, but which the youngsters had no choice but to wear.

The second year that John and I were dropped from the fixture we were made to score and umpire. My stint of umpiring led to no Rustic wickets, and was not popular with the ever-pressing Dumplings. John's turn as scorer was chaotic. Order was only saved by the fact that the Dumplings had someone who was able to count at the same time as watching the cricket.

On the third year, we were ready to circumvent the perils of a Rustic day off. I had brought the canoe on tour, strapped to the top of the Skoda, and we crawled in humble supplication to our captain, who is the senior Crazey's nephew, to beg time out to put the boat into the river Exe. Permission was granted. Robert Pinney, who was with The Rustics for the day, took a particular interest in our plan, claiming to have taken part in the annual Exe raft race. He thought our assertion that we would rejoin the cricketers for lunch was a bit ambitious, given the timings of our plan. We told him we knew what we were doing and would have time to spare, but I raised an eyebrow at John.

Robert was the son of George Pinney, who for many years was the gracious and tolerant host of our tour. With all things Rustic rooted in farming, this George was also a farmer. He and his wife, Dawn, generously opened up their rambling home at Horn Park to the ravages of the Rustics for a week each July. Every year we would be taken to see his large dairy herd and we would invariably receive an update on relations between the farm and the neighbour who had some large trout ponds. They were not well located, being downhill of George's slurry lagoon. Crazey always avoided the farm walk, as being a computer expert, he had once been asked by George to fix a glitch on the cow record system. He had succeeded in erasing all of the cow data and had spent a nerve-wracking day trying to recover it, without George knowing what was happening.

Breakfast at Horn Park was an institution run by the kindly and tolerant Dawn, who would rise at the "crack of" in order to feed her horses before setting out the breakfast table. Her speciality, to save time, was to fry the eggs early and then reheat when the hung-over and unruly Rustics came to the table. We learnt quickly to opt, gratefully, for these rubberized eggs, for the alternative was worse: antique cereals. George would return from the dairy with a small churn containing milk. A shrewd farmer, he believed that the best milk should be sold, not wasted on his young guests. Once, and that was enough, we discovered that what was actually in the can was waste milk, stripped from a mastitic cow, and therefore of a pungent pink consistency. On one morning the Cornflakes and Frosties were subjected to an age inspection, and the youngest packet was found to be seven years past its use-by-date. Very little cereal was ever consumed, so of course the packets returned to the cellars in readiness for the following year. Only new recruits ever had a bowl of cereal and we always enjoyed such a moment, knowing they would have to be polite, as Dawn would be in the kitchen with us during the meal. We suspected it would cause trouble if she was notified of George's food gathering decisions. Watching the unwary new boys pushing the clotted blood and mouldy flakes around their bowls while looking polite was a source of much mirth to us older Rustics.

George was a traditional sporting farmer, playing cricket five days a week. He was also a JP, who dispensed justice on the Dorset bench on days off. He hunted all winter and was a Master of the Cattistock fox hounds. We all suspected that his cowman did not know who he was. Tragically, George had a hunting accident, which paralysed him and so caused him to sell the business to a farm management company before he passed away, a year after the injury. Robert, his son, was thus redundant for a period. As an unemployed farmer, therefore, we concluded that Robert genuinely would have had time to raft down the Exe and that his comment about us missing lunch was quite likely to be true. We were keen that our captain, Crazey junior, did not have this same information.

Sam, a Rustic who came from Lancashire, agreed to drive the Skoda to Bampton, just north of Tiverton, and to drop us in the river. Accompanied by Dickon, who is one of the nicest Rustics, they then dropped the Skoda off at a pub called the Fisherman's Cot, below the famed bridge at Bickleigh. It is famed because it is not the bridge in the song "Bridge Over Troubled Water." It is, nonetheless, a wonderful, ancient, curving and gracefully-arched construction, through which the river tumbles over the weir stones, and has served to make the pub a popular tourist destination.

July is a gorgeous time on the river, where the cool water running off the moors and the shade of a mix of mature trees along the river bank combine to create a dappled haven from the heat. The Exe is a clean river in its middle reach and the splintering sunlight lit the large pebbles of the river bed through the shimmers of the shallow water.

We had an idyllic paddle down towards Tiverton, the only incident occurring when portageing a weir. John was pulling the canoe along the bank above a frothy little fish ladder when he lost his footing. Into water went man and boat, the canoe sinking rather quickly as it wedged into the cascading steps of the ladder. A lady walking her dog on the river bank joined me in laughing heartily at John's clumsiness.

We canoed into Tiverton, where we enjoyed the sight of its tall church tower reaching upwards elegantly from the wooded river edge and stopped to buy a cold drink. While in the town centre, John met another woman who invited him on an impromptu guided tour of the Town Hall, a beautifully ornamented and surprisingly grand civic building. I missed out on the tour, as I had popped into a bookshop. I spent the half hour of his disappearance vaguely wondering where he had got to this time.

We portaged the Town Rapids, a potentially exciting bit of white water flowing over a large oblique weir, as there was too little water for it to be worthwhile, and then on to Bickleigh, having to drag the boat through several shallow deposits of river pebbles. At Bickleigh we dropped over the weir and into the pool below the bridge, onto which the pub's shady gardens spilled.

Our journey had been brief, perhaps around two and a half hours, as we had promised to return to the County Ground in Exeter for cricketing duties. These could include scoring, umpiring or certain embarrassing shopping duties. The river was cool, the pub hospitable and our spirits high after a perfect little paddle. We decided to stop for lunch. A further two and a half hours passed during which we had a memorable Hole and Dinnis (Smith and Jones) talking heads session. We explored at great length which historical figures we would like to have been.

At first I had chosen Joseph, of the Technicolour Dreamcoat, as he was a wise agricultural planner, had a difficult start and an interesting liaison with the wife of Potiphar. I thought that by the end of his life he would have been a proud and wise man, responsible for saving the Egyptians from the ravages of famine and drought. Then I settled upon the Director of Conservation for the Bialowieza primeval forest at the time it became Poland's first National Park in 1921, in response to the total loss of free living Bison in the country. I have visited these vast tranquil forests and was awe struck by the completeness of nature within their unmanaged interior. The scale of challenge faced by conservationists in Poland, after the horror of the wars, was enormous but had been tackled with bravura spirit. Their reverence for the wilderness was deep and palpable. I argued that a man capable of saving the forests in that era was truly a great conservationist. During my visit I had enjoyed a memorable May midnight in the forest and had managed to call up an eagle owl, Bubo bubo, by impersonating a rival. The sound of this regal ruler of the night brought the forest quaking from its star-lit stillness. I had imagined this King of the Night perched in a giant tree, framed against the galaxy above, issuing a powerful owlish decree.

"I'd love to hear that," said John. I obliged, with my best effort. It is a sound not too different from the threatening grumble of a lion, designed to assert dominance of territory and irresistible sexual power. It is a noise that comes from the animal soul. I got the call out to perfection. John told me he had meant the real thing and not my impersonation, which had also attracted the attention of some of the pub's other guests. I had wanted to tell him about a research project in the forest on the dispersal of tree seeds, but it seemed the time to return to the Rustics had arrived.

The Exe rises on Exmoor only five miles from the Bristol Channel, but then flows due south to the big, muddy estuary below Exeter, on Devon's south coast. This illogical long way round was probably caused when the great masses of rock beneath the Exmoor peat tipped and buckled, as seismic forces exerted their powerful forces millions of years ago, tilting southwards and allowing the rivers to erode their headwaters northwards against the river flow. From the moor, the descent of the water is steep and rapid, and cuts through dramatic scenery dominated by the hills of hard red sandstone.

Flowing from the peat its water is slightly acidic, deterring sea trout, but providing some excellent runs of salmon. The name derives from the Latin word isca, which means "water filled with fish", and the Exe shares this derivation with the Axe, the Esk and the Usk. It is, thus, in good company.

When canoeing the Arun we had met some interesting men in a pub who may have been experts in local history, but not in river trivia. Their assertion that the Arun discharges more water into the English Channel than any other on the South Coast was quite wrong. It may be the biggest in Sussex, though The Ouse may give it a good run for its money, but its average discharge is only a third of that flowing out of The Exe, which in spate disgorges six times as much water as The Arun in flood. This can make it a very interesting river to canoe when the moor is wet and the water is up, which planted the seed of an idea.

"John, I've got a plan," I said a month or so after our return home from the tour. "I've got a farming meeting in Cornwall, in November, so why don't we make a trip of it and do The Exe on the way down? It should be an interesting challenge then, as the waters will be running."

John came down with George, not Pinney but farmer Hosford, and I arrived with a trailer and two canoes. It was the third week of November, the October rains had been massive and ceased only a few days before our arrival. Our meeting place was the Fisherman's Cot at Bickleigh, the scene of our previous engagement with the river. This time we intended a longer journey, from just below Dulverton back down to where we were staying, at The Cot.

I had taken the liberty of inviting a fourth farmer to join the adventure. Steve was one of a group of 20 farmers who had all attended the 2004 refresher course in Farm Management sponsored by The Worshipful Company of Farmers, held at Wye, where I had first met him. I recall saying of George that his beautiful and intricately-managed farm was a reflection of his soul. That is also a good starting point in trying to describe the mighty character that is Steve. He farms a large arable acreage in Northamptonshire and is passionate about his soils and the life that should lie therein. Large woods divide his fields and the Great Ouse flows through his meadows, but the real description of him lies in his granaries. They are enormous and filled to overflowing. Great stores with the doors open and massive piles of fat grain spilling out. The same holds for the vast silage pits filled to bursting with maize and red clover for a fine herd of beef cattle. The scale of his production is enormous, and is rooted in his fascination with soil quality. He is a champion of the importance of the earth worm. He is the physical manifestation of this vision of fertile plenty, a man mountain, great fun and full of mischief.

Steve had come to stay at Montague when my girls were small. They had greatly enjoyed what they thought was his impersonation of a bear, but was in fact the noise he normally emitted while sleeping. When he left the farm he was forever after known as "Daddy's New Bear Friend," or NBF for short. He had made the error of asking me "if there was ever a spare seat in the canoe, could he come on one of our adventures?" He did not need to ask more than once, as I have always enjoyed his company. On our arrival at The Cot, larger than life, Steve was there to greet us. The crew was gathered, a pleasant supper was had and we went late to bed in preparation for the excitement of the day to come.

I was first to wake, before dawn, and made myself unpopular with George, John, NBF and the breakfast chef by insisting that "we need to get going." After breakfast we had our first inspection of the river. The crew went quiet.

"Didn't look like this in July," said John, looking slightly puzzled. He had to raise his voice to be heard above the roar of the river.

"You are not seriously going to canoe in that, are you?" said Steve, pointing at The Exe thundering over the weir beneath the bridge. He was wearing his "onesie" of bike leathers.

"You are not seriously going to canoe in that, are you?" I replied, jabbing at the bike leathers. "I told you to get a wet suit or a dry suit."

"Well, I had a look on the internet, and the only place in the world with a wet suit big enough for me was in New York," Steve said. "But don't worry, these are really warm. And I'm definitely not going to go into the water, now that I've had a look at it." John looked at him with a mixture of pity and amusement.

We set off to our pre-arranged launch point, a hotel by a bridge at the point where the river leaves the moorland of the National Park. The kindly hotelier had agreed to us parking in his car park for the day, having told us that The Exe had flooded a couple of years ago and reached the second floor of his building. We looked around the narrow valley, trying to conceive the catastrophic scale of such a flood. It was good to have that image in our minds, as the river was running about an inch below a level described as "high flow" on a gauge attached to the bridge. It gave us a sense of perspective. At least the river wasn't really, really, angry. There was a frost and a thin mist, misleadingly peaceful, hung about the valley. Feeble tendrils of sun were trying to penetrate from above. The scene was beautifully set for our much anticipated adventure.

John and George efficiently set off first from the bank, and swiftly sped to the other side. I stepped into our canoe and steadied it for the loading of NBF. He eventually sat down, in the middle seat of the boat, and I had my first doubts of the morning. The boat can easily take three adults of average weight. My load now consisted of two adults, one of whom was more than double the bulk of an average human. I now realised why John and George had sped to the other side of the river like two naughty moorhens. George wanted a photograph. John had obviously calculated what the effect of NBF would be on the canoe and instructed George to get camera ready. The picture he took shows the two of us seated in the canoe, with the boat sitting impossibly low in the water. We are smiling at the camera, unaware of just how little freeboard we have. It explains the events of the next two hours.

The river was quite noisy and there was going to be a lot of white-water during the day. However, the first few hundred yards were enchantingly peaceful. Through the mist we could see a herd of deer, who seemed unfazed by the canoes going past. This resembled a peaceful vision of Eden, and I began a discourse on the beauty of Exmoor, and the loveliness of the English seasons. NBF was a fellow enthusiast, and highly appreciative of our setting. The dreamy conversation quickly proved to be an unhelpful distraction from our mission, and I failed to notice the large rock, in the middle of the speeding river. Coupled with my lack of attentiveness to the quickly moving water, the canoe was proving very difficult to steer, so we hit the rock hard. It was enough to tip the canoe over.

As the water swamped the boat I swam out to one side and held on to the canoe by its rope. NBF was wearing a life jacket, so the fact that he had sunk without trace did not at first concern me. The water was running powerfully and something strange was now happening beneath its broiling surface. A huge black mound was rising from the water, rather like one of those volcanic islands that periodically emerge from the South Pacific. I could discern the air filled buttocks of the bike leathers glistening in the weak sun light. After the bottom, thankfully, the head was next to rise from the Exe. The life jacket, having eventually equalised buoyancy with the inflated bike leathers, finally succeeded in raising the critical parts of my friend to the surface. I mused only briefly on the source of all this air, feeling that any questions to NBF about whether he had supplied it himself might not go down very well. He slowly got his bearings and looked over to me, grinning much like a walrus which has just caught a salmon. He was relishing the experience.

We reorganised our boat and set off on our way again. John and George were some way ahead and we were glad that our upset had not been witnessed. They were in an odiously smug mood. NBF remained cheerful, and we continued to enjoy the splendid scenery along the river. After another mile or so we came to a dilapidated steel bridge, the water swirling angrily through and round its stanchions. One route was blocked by a fallen tree and piles of debris, but a route to the left looked viable if we could negotiate a tight right hand turn immediately below the bridge.

John and George were pulled up on the bank just below the bridge. They, clearly, had only just succeeded in making the turn, and thought a good photo opportunity may be about to occur. George already had his camera pointing at the bridge. In a later discussion we decided that this was rather annoying.

We made it through the choppy water of the left hand channel, and NBF let out a whoop and a holler of delight. Our triumph was short lived, however, and we failed to make the tight turn in the chasing current below the wrecked bridge. The canoe capsized again and, being a bit more nimble than NBF, I was able to grab the bank, and avoid submergence. NBF once again completely disappeared beneath the water, into a deep scour at the bottom of the tumultuous water. I knew I would be unable to lift him if I found him, which I couldn't. He had tumbled down the channel some distance before finally surfacing like a courting leviathan. Not since the days of the mighty dinosaurs had The Exe witnessed such a creature, I thought to myself.

John and George thanked us for the entertainment and disappeared downstream without offering to help. They had the gallingly self-satisfied and superior air that people sometimes have when dealing with a couple of incompetents. I was fully aware that the photos, proof of their current attitude, were to become cherished trophies of George's day. NBF also sensed this increasingly competitive relationship and we resolved to catch our friends in as elegant a fashion as possible.

The frost had still not left the floor of the valley and the rime persisted in the pockets of slope and wood not yet touched by the weak morning sun. The temperature was not yet above freezing. Conversation, of which NBF was not usually short, had been replaced by a chilly determination. Neither of us wanted to go in again, so we were coordinating well, descending the rapids with concentrated effort and clear communication about which side to paddle and how fast. For a while we worked successfully, but then another bridge loomed from around another corner. This was a nicer bridge than the previous steel wreck, gracefully arching over the swift current in two attractively stone worked spans. Debris filled one span completely, but a gap in the left span was just about wide enough for the canoe to pass through. This course was going to take us perilously close to an overhanging tree. So perilously, in fact, that NBF made the gross error of grabbing hold of the offending branch as we paddled beneath. It lifted his majestic figure entirely from the middle seat and into the air, a nanosecond before I, still in the seat behind, cannoned into the back of him. The canoe slid swiftly from under us and we both entered the water for a third time.

We clambered out and again went through the laborious process of rescuing the boat. I revealed my thoughts to NBF, who began to look slightly miffed when I observed that he had so wonderfully morphed from a South Pacific volcano, via walrus and whale to gorilla. Not correctly reading the expression on his face, I continued in the vein I was in, suggesting that his journey resembled the origins of life and the course of evolution to Homo sapiens. He made a harrumph of a response that "a day's pheasant shooting would be a lot more comfortable." He knew I would not think highly of such an assertion, so we hurried on our way, both of us beginning to feel the cold.

There were two more bridges to get under and we succeeded in not capsizing only on the last of them. We were both getting really cold by this point, although I was rather more sensibly dressed than NBF. His fleece lined leathers were no longer keeping him warm and they probably weighed an extra two stone, saturated as they were. We stopped on the bank having eventually caught up with George and John, who appeared to have stopped for a little nap. There we changed into some dry clothes, hiding from George, whose camera was out again, and then paddled carefully into the little Devon town of Tiverton for lunch.

Through the middle of Tiverton the river runs through ugly concrete flood banks, half way along which are the Town Rapids. This is an interesting descent in the right conditions, although on our visit in the summer the water flow had been insufficient for us to canoe down the rapid. After lunch, we had an inspection of the falls. The river was pouring down them now, and they looked an interesting challenge. NBF had made his mind up that shooting pheasants really was more civilized than shooting rapids. Resolving to stay warm and dry, he had volunteered to return to Dulverton in a taxi to collect the Land Rover and trailer, leaving me to canoe down to Bickleigh on my own. The morning's adventure had satisfied his desire for joining me in the canoe and he said he "really wouldn't mind never venturing out with me in a canoe ever again," but that he would remain in Tiverton long enough to watch John and I descent the rapid, each alone in our canoes. He and George filmed our descent, which was much easier than it looked, and the sound track includes the sound of NBF hollering in excitement as we made it to the flat river at the end of the run. Despite the discomfort of his morning's journery, our friendship remained intact.

For the afternoon I had the rare treat of paddling on my own. The sensitivity of the boat had fully recovered with the absence of NBF, so I had an exhilarating run down to the famous bridge at the Fishermans Cot. Canoeists talk of the song of the paddle and this part of our journey was a melody in tune with the river. I enjoyed the technical challenge of the boat in the river as well as the ease of steerage without a committee process.

I also had a plan. It occured to me that the weir under the famous bridge was actually quite a tricky obstacle, especially given the strength of the current. With only me in the boat it would be a doddle, but I reckoned John and George might have a problem. George looked smart, like an old pro in his colourful dry suite, and was still taking the mickey over my morning's dousings. I don't ever wish people ill, but I did want to be in a good position below the weir when John and George came down.

After my wonderful afternoon on the river I capped it off with a quite elegant drop down the weir and a consummately neat turn directly below the bridge so that I could sit in an eddy and watch the attempt by John and George. My newly acquired smugness was reinforced by applause from an audience of elderly walkers on the pub lawn. The scene was perfectly set.

The bridge had five arches. John and George chose wrongly. They came through the one with the biggest amount of water going through, and I licked my lips with a satanic anticipation. As their boat sloped to go down the face of the rocks the river gave a crocolilian shrug, lifting the back of their boat off line. It tipped sideways, filled immediately with the River Exe and sank. John went under completely, a seal disappearing beneath the waves. George, who has an irrational fear of being submerged in the river, comleted a feat of gymnastic impossibility, and took off over the water like a colourful, but demented, lily trotter. He left his partner in the water and from the bank instructed him to rescue the boat on his own. he wasn't about to get any wetter. I laughed at the indignity of their predicament so much that I lost my place in the eddy and was swept down river another hundred yards before I could land.

He who laught last.....

NBF

Afloat

The Dee in spate after journey

Teepee on the Wye

An old ruin on the Wye

John on the town rapids Tiverton

Beavers

Dinnisiae

The Canche

Another portage

The Cuckmere

Chapter 9
The Swale - August 2013

Narrated by John

The Swale is not, technically, a river. It is an estuary connecting estuaries. However, it is sometimes called the River Swale, which would have been accurate sometime back in geological time. This leads to further confusion, as there is another River Swale that comes off the Yorkshire Dales where a six foot annual rainfall causes a very rapid stream to deluge along its course into The Ure and then The Ouse. The Ouse joins in the river-naming fun, as there are five of them in the UK, and there are also five River Stours. Five River Fromes are joined by four River Dees. The Avon probably takes the prize, there being eight in Britain, with the Welsh Avon being called the Afon Afan just to make things clearer. There are two River Rothers, in Sussex, and there are two River Axes in adjacent counties, Devon and Somerset, one of which, aptly, emerges from the giant underwater lakes of Wookey Hole. I should also point out that the River Arun we had canoed in Sussex had a sister in the Himalayas called the River Arun. It would seem that naming a river is not as complex as defining one.

Our Swale separates the Isle of Sheppey from its North Kent mainland, and links the mouth of the Medway to the Greater Thames. At low tide it is a glorious glistening expanse of rich silt containing millions of shell fish and other invertebrates on which large numbers of waders and wildfowl feed. At high tide the sea rises, completely covering the expanse of mudflats. It swells to a level above the height of the fringing marshes, which are protected by sea walls made from clay and faced with ragstone, a hard limestone quarried from the North Downs chalk. The transformation between high and low tide is not just dramatic, it is also very quick, and the currents can be very dangerous. There are many stories of boating tragedies and drowning in the Swale, but in the right conditions it can provide some interesting canoeing. Martin was keen to meet up, for another summer holiday outing with all of our children, to gently paddle and see the seals on the sand-banks off Shellness, on the north shore at the mouth of the estuary.

Recently I had heard an amusing story about the Whitstable Oyster Farm, just along from the Swale. The piscatology student had parked a tractor, used for bringing in the shell fish, in the wrong place below the high tide mark. It had flotation tyres for driving on the mud flats, and with an east wind and an ascending tide the tractor had literally floated away up the Swale. It was found several miles from its parking spot on the following morning, in perfect working order. This confirmed in my mind that strange things happened on this coastline.

This desire to go for a paddle in an estuary came as something of a surprise to me, as Martin did not usually want to go anywhere near the sea in his canoes, citing excuses about having the wrong sort of boat and the water not being our friend. I asked why he had changed his mind.

"I think that if we catch the water either side of high tide then we can go with the flow in both directions. If there is no wind, we can cross safely from the ferry at Oare, on the south side, at the narrowest point, and creep along the coast to get a view of the seals, on the sand banks a mile or so to the north east. Oh, and just to be safe, I will bring my brother."

I knew Patrick, Martin's brother, from having played cricket with him. He was a less athletic and an even more eccentric and impractical version of his older brother, though at an academic level probably brighter. However, I did not associate "safety" in any way, shape or form with him. In fact, I reckoned he could only add to the chaos. Not unusually, I was unable to imagine what was going through Martin's mind but, as per normal, agreed to a rendezvous for the expedition.

I must mention that Patrick had recently had a bicycle accident, while riding past Buckingham Palace. He woke in hospital, with a dislocated hip, and, being a solicitor, had the immediate thought that the upside of his predicament would at least be a big cheque extorted through the courts from the driver who had knocked him over. In a witness statement from a taxi driver, read to him by a policeman, the following information was gleaned. That a "posh-looking geezer on a kid's bike wobbling like a weeble" hit the kerb and fell off with no one anywhere near him. The news was worse, for not only would no suing take place, but the doctors had discovered that he actually needed two new hips. Years of being flat footed had worn out both joints. He did, ruefully, admit to his brother that the bike accident had been preceded by a "damn good lunch" with one of his City mates.

Martin and I arrived at the slipway at Oare, just outside Faversham on the Kent coast, at the same time. I brought the triplets, George and his friend Henry and a single, rather ancient, kayak. Martin arrived with three canoes on his trailer. Twenty minutes later, Patrick arrived in a separate vehicle, towing a large rib, an inflatable boat with an enormous outboard engine, muttering heatedly about having had to follow a "bloody farmer" in a tractor. A total of five boats, three adults and eight children thus assembled on the slipway of the old Harty ferry, by the nature reserve at Oare.

The tide was perfect, approaching the slack at the peak of high water, and the sun was shining. The rib was launched, with an enormous amount of meaningless banter between the two brothers. All the children wanted to go in the rib, but there was only room enough for two at a time. Martin complained bitterly when Patrick opened the throttle and roared into the middle of the estuary, giving all of the children turns at speedy joy riding.

"What a disaster," he moaned "I don't know why I asked him to come. That vulgar boat will scare away all the wildlife. It's loud and dirty and smelly..." Fortunately, he then ran out of words.

Eventually the excitement of the rib was dampened. Most of the children were given places in the canoes, and told to stick together in a tight formation to cross the dangerous narrow of The Swale. However, we had lost some time and the ebb tide was beginning to race. This was not apparent in the shelter of the shoreline where we launched, but about 50 metres off shore the water was ripping out to sea. We could tell this because the canoes, captained by the children who had beetled away from the launch site, were scattered across The Swale in no formation whatsoever. The little craft were being whistled briskly away to the dangers of the North Sea. Our orders for them to stick closely together had been totally ignored and, rather suddenly, a calamity began to unfold. The children themselves did not appear to realise the danger they were in, so were paddling rapidly ever further into the peril.

"This isn't very clever," we said to each other in unison. We watched the situation from our own canoe and shouted at the child in the single kayak and the others in the other two canoes, to get back to shore immediately. This advice, also, was ignored, though the noise of the rib may have drowned out our increasingly desperate shouting. Or maybe it was the wind, which had blown up suddenly and was whipping the estuary surface into a short and awkward chop.

At the same moment we both thought that Patrick might actually become useful. He was still showing off the rib, obliviously describing circles at full throttle in the middle of The Swale. We started waving to attract his attention. His rib went from circles to figures of eight, with no diminution of speed. Eventually Romney, one of his passengers, tapped him on the shoulder and pointed towards Martin and I waving impotently but vigorously with both arms from our little boat. He throttled down, passing the endangered children in the three disappearing canoes, and came over to us, not realising that most of our precious offspring were in the tragic act of becoming lost at sea.

He was instructed, tersely, to make himself useful by going back out into the estuary to rescue the errant young canoeists, which he succeeded in doing really rather efficiently. Martin and I were both surprised at this efficiency, and very, very, relieved.

"Thank goodness for Patrick," said Martin, before adding, with the sort of ingratitude only a brother could summon, "I think I've waited nearly fifty years to say that!"

We re-gathered on the slipway and changed our plan. It was possible to find slack water along the lee of the sea wall and to follow the shore line up to the sheltered inlet of Oare creek. This was only a journey of about a mile, but was made interesting by the fact that it harboured some wonderful Thames barges and that The Shipwrights Arms, a characterful old pub, could be accessed at the top of the creek. We re-allocated the children to various craft, two of them getting into the rib with Patrick, and took our fleet on the gentle run to the creek. The sun was hot and we could just about stay out of the wind, so we made good progress towards lunch. Just before reaching our destination, we were greeted by two seals who were most curious about the flotilla invading their territory and put on a good show. The children were thrilled as this was their first ever encounter with seals. Martin thought that this was adequate to claim that the main objective of the mission had been achieved.

The rib was well ahead of us and we had hoped that Patrick would have gone ahead to get lunch ordered. As we neared the pub, which was on the quayside, we could see the rib wallowing in the middle of the creek with its mighty outboard silent. It didn't look quite right. I paddled up to the boat and was greeted by Patrick looking hot and bothered. He was trying to lift the outboard motor out of the water, but it seemed to have become stuck. In fact, each time he tried to tilt the engine the front of his boat gave a downward jerk. There was an odd see saw action going on which, I soon diagnosed, was caused by the painter secured to the front of the rib. Florence had accidentally dropped it into the sea while approaching the mooring and it had become snarled around the propeller. Patrick seemed to share his brother's mechanical aptitude. Martin then arrived in his canoe and, unhelpfully, asked him why he hadn't got the food sorted out. "Because I have got my propeller caught in a rope," came the irritated response. I knew that Martin would be useless at sorting out this problem, so I took off my life jacket and dived under the rib to see how bad the problem was. With the use of a knife, it took less than five minutes to untangle the rope and to free the rib. It was Patrick's turn to be grateful.

Patrick's gratitude was soon put to good effect by his brother who, upon having ordered a slap up lunch for eight hungry children and three adults, announced that he hadn't bought his wallet. I had made the same careful provision, so poor Patrick would have to pick up the sizeable bill. Lunch was one of those special, happy summer family outings. We were a very merry crew, thoroughly enjoying our adventure.

There is a very good reason why I have written up the Swale escapade. Martin had spent six happy years working on the Elmley National Nature Reserve, helping Philip Merricks with the challenge. He was proud of this phase of his life and had adored his time on the marshes. I know that were he to have written this chapter we would be faced with lengthy descriptions of the wildlife of this extraordinary place. His love of lapwings would be given full reign and I suspect he would also be giving us the story of the European white fronted geese, arriving on the east wind from the Arctic tundra on a December moonlit night, calling with voices of winter joy. He was chuntering about some species of sea grass in the salt marshes which, he told the children, "had arrived in Southampton Water on the Queen Mary's bottom and then spread everywhere," when, fortunately, his attention was diverted by an immaculately restored Thames barge. It was called the Mimosa which, while we sat in the sun after lunch, led Martin to relate the following tale.

> "The Mimosa is a Victorian sailing barge, owned by a rather interesting old sea dog called Captain Dodds. The barge is available for commercial hire and in the autumn last year he had chartered it to Philip, who had kindly invited me and, more importantly, Potto, my father-in-law, to come with him for the day's cruise up and down the Swale. Potto was not in the best of health and was well into his eighties, but had been an intrepid sailor in his younger days, and Philip, also a keen sailor, had been one of his crew on several of these adventures. The two men enjoyed each other's company. I went along to look after Potto, and to enjoy the trip on the boat and the views of birdlife that I would gain in the middle of the Swale. The age of the sailing barge was a golden phase in the history of industrial transport and these easy to sail and shallow drafted ships, often crewed only by the skipper and a boy, were masterpieces of boat design. If hundreds of thousands of tons of cargo each year could be moved by wind power, and without pollution, in and out of one of the world's busiest cities today, it would be considered a marvellous ecological and technical achievement, but sadly the age of the

barge has passed. This is another example of answers to human needs provided by rivers being ignored by our society."

"Where is this story going?" asked Patrick, ever the younger brother, and clearly used to lengthy rambling discourses from his elder.

"Well, it is a story about a horse, actually," Martin responded, rather surprisingly, though he continued on the subject of the barge:

> "While pottering about on the deck of the Mimosa, John had tripped over a large horizontal pole, to which the mainsail was attached, called a "horse." I only just grabbed the old boy before he pitched into the hold. No harm was done, but, I told Philip, this was not the first time he had fallen from a horse. Potto had been a keen hunting man and a very good rider, and when I first married Gundrada he had bought a horse called George. Potto was the sort of man who took little notice of the opinions of others and had bought the horse without veterinary advice. George was a big, raw-boned and wholly uncoordinated creature whose lungs were shot, whose tendons were fired, who was blind in one eye and who had been retired early from racing due to an unsound temperament, an uncontrollable gallop and an inability to jump. Of course, it was love at first sight."

"Is this story going to take all day?" asked Patrick, interrupting once again. He seemed keen to get his brother to the point. Martin ignored him and carried on:

> "On this particular morning Gundrada, Potto and I were going to exercise the horses over the farm. He was the first to mount and as he climbed on to the beloved steed, a troop of guinea fowl appeared in the yard. This was too much for George who bolted, skittering over the cobbles and leaping the yard gate as he fled. There was a "clink" as I thought his back heels touched the top rail, but it turned out to be the reins and bridle catching on the scroll work of the gate and being ripped from George's head. The horse then headed down the drive towards the cattle grid and towards the busy road through the village, with Potto clinging to

its mane, having lost all ability to steer or to stop his mount. He approached the cattle grid, which has parallel steel bars that would surely snap the horse's legs and catapult Potto to certain death. For the second time in a matter of seconds George the horse proved his ex-trainer wholly wrong about his jumping ability and cleared the grid in a graceful leap and, still defying the experience of the ex-trainer, hit his galloping stride immediately on landing the other side. Potto was a very gentle man, but could now be seen reaching forward to punch George in the head with his left fist, in an effort to steer the runaway into the comparative safety of the field, away from the road. He punched George in his good eye, until he eventually responded, veering into the open field, still at top speed."

"Once in the field, Potto decided to dismount sliding from the saddle and off the side of the still galloping George. He hit the ground with an awful crunch. Potto carried his pen knife on a long shoelace attached to his belt, and George managed to put his hind leg through this loop, and dragged him along the ground. Showing the strength and stamina that had eluded previous owners, the run-away horse continued at a gallop. At this point Gundrada and I were running towards the unfolding drama and as we arrived on the scene the bootlace broke and horse and rider became separate entities. In front of us lay the crumpled heap of Potto's battered body. Gundrada was becoming rather emotional, while I was hoping his will was in order. We both expected him to be a thoroughly broken corpse."

"How long does this story go on for?" asked Patrick.

"Not long, but the lovely bit is yet to come," replied Martin.

"As we got to Potto, he stood up, like Lazarus. Badly shaken, he gave us both a seraphic smile and said with enthusiasm, 'What a horse! You could point him at anything!' "

It seemed this amusing story was finally at an end, so Patrick paid for the meal, and we got back into the various boats to paddle back to the slipway where our vehicles were parked. We arrived back there without mishap, although son George's friend, Henry, in the single kayak, decided to ignore advice and paddled towards the middle of the estuary, where the strength of the ebb tide carried him backwards until he found quieter water.

On arriving at the slipway we noticed that things had changed considerably. The water was about a hundred metres from the shore and the glistening muds were being rapidly revealed. The slipway would only be operational for another quarter of an hour. This did not matter to the canoeist, but was critical for the landing of the rib.

Patrick's day had started well, with the rescue, but had drifted into more characteristic terrain with his mix up with the painter and the collection of the bill for lunch. This downward spiral looked to be continuing, as he was standing in the sea beside his rib, looking perplexed, as we were just returning to the slipway.

"Are you O.K.?" asked Martin.

"No," he replied rather sorrowfully, "the rib is stuck in the mud and I can't move it at all."

Martin and I wandered over to the stuck boat and, after a brief inspection, agreed with his observation.

"Yep. She is good and stuck," said Martin. "But the high tide should refloat her.... in, oooh, about seven hours."

He and I then put our shoulder under the rib and pushed hard, dislodging her slightly, and slowly, with much effort shunted her towards the slip way. It was arduous work and, for some reason, Patrick was not helping us with the task. Realising we were running out of time for getting the boat safely out of the water, we simply carried on shoving. Despite teasing Patrick, we did not want it to be left stranded on the mud flats by the departing tide. Only once we had gained the slipway did we realise why Patrick had got the boat stuck. He had left the engine down and none of us had realised. There was a plough line in the mud gouged by the projecting propeller.

"Can you please lend us a hand moving your ship, instead of just standing there doing nothing," Martin called to Patrick, who appeared to have gone into a trance, standing in the thigh high water while his brother and I had heaved the rib to a secure position on the slipway.

"I can't, I'm stuck," came the forlorn response.

We returned from the slipway to inspect Patrick in the mud of the estuary. I looked carefully at his predicament, and then at Martin. If women marry men in their father's image, then I could see why Gundrada had married Martin. He had the seraphic smile on his face of the cat that got the cream, the same smile that Potto wore after surviving the fall from his horse.

"And I am sinking," added Patrick showing ever increasing signs of misery. Martin's smile broadened still further. Despite his rotundity, Patrick was not built for buoyancy. He was indeed sinking and the water was up over his shorts, nearly waist high. We surmised that his new hips were not really up to the job of extricating the remainder of the body from the stinking silt. As the tide was falling, this meant that he was actually going downwards into the mud.

"We shall have to lift him carefully," said Martin, still grinning wolfishly, but with a little bit of sympathy, because he was actually quite fond of his brother. We each got under an arm and gently tried to prize him from the sucking ooze. It was not a straight forward mission, as in trying to lever the great mass upwards we found, instead, that we were both pushing our own selves down into the sinking mud. After much struggling we succeeded in re-floating him. He was covered in black, stinking slime up to his waist, but was grateful to be mobile again. Martin and I were both in our wet suits, so were easily able to clean ourselves in the rapidly ebbing estuary. Not so Patrick, who still had on his shorts, in the pocket of which, unfortunately, was his most precious possession.

Looking stricken, he then asked where the boat trailer had been put. It was not where it had been left. Unknown to us, Julie had unhitched it from Patrick's car and taken it with her to Henry's parents house, on a nearby strawberry farm, to keep it safe, and meanwhile had got stuck behind another tractor on her way back to Oare to collect us. She eventually arrived, which elicited from Patrick some ungrateful comments, mainly about "bloody farmers."

"Any one seen my phone?" he then asked, before reaching down to his soaked silt-filled pocket. His phone had not survived the immersion in the ooze, perfectly rounding off his experience of a canoeing adventure with the two farmers.

Chapter 10
A little river called The Rhiw - January 2014

By Martin

As a result of our experience on the Exe and the afternoon of paddling a canoe on my own on some Grade Three rapids, I suggested to John that we were ready for a proper white-water river adventure. I said it would be fun to take one canoe each and really test ourselves. He agreed, adding that just the two of us should go. Inadvertently he had stumbled onto the correct allocation of man to canoe. Things were looking good.

I ordered some maps of the River Dee. We chatted about getting down some rapids near Llangollen called the Serpents Tail and the Horseshoe Falls. This was exciting stuff. We watched film of kayakers athletically breasting these famous bits of water.

The rain had been heavy all winter. News film showed flooded landscapes all over the south of England. The Abbey at Tewkesbury on the Severn, marooned on its knoll above the floodwaters, the inland sea of the Somerset Levels and even homes along The Thames being inundated were but a few of the haunting media images. A tragedy in which a kayakist drowned on the River Usk made me think more carefully about our plan. It was a sodden, sombre January.

I phoned John. He blamed the flooding across the country on the wind pump I had recently installed on the farm. This was a great project undertaken to relieve summer drought on our marshlands. It was designed to keep our wetlands wet and our ditches topped up with water to fence the cattle and sheep in the right fields. The pump worked perfectly, but as it had rained ever since it had been built, it looked rather absurd, pulling water into already flooded pastures. It is not uncommon on farms to discover well-thought through and executed plans entirely undone by the vagaries of nature.

Having discussed farming, the phone conversation then turned to the expedition. "I am not sure about the Dee," I said.

"In fact, I am," I then said with involuntary decisiveness, before John could get a word in.

John, understandably, was confused at the other end of the line. Somehow, sub-consciously, I grieved for the man who had died on the Usk, and the months of rain had washed some of my usual enthusiasm away.

"What I mean is I think we should find a smaller river. I have one in mind, a little tributary of the Severn, which rises in the hills above Welshpool. It will be fun and a lot safer."

While a river rhou is a small fish plentiful in the sacred Ganges, the river Rhiw, pronounced identically, is a spate river rising in the foot hills of the Cambrian Mountains in mid Wales and flows into the mighty Severn. At the river junction is the little village of Berriew, our equivalent of Namche Bazaar, where friends of mine and Gundrada had recently bought a small castle. One more phone call to our friends at Berriew and we had supper, bed and breakfast organised. We agreed to meet there on Sunday evening, in three days time, and do the river on the Monday. The plan was under way.

John and I had recently watched an old documentary of a remarkable canoe story. The Ganges has its headwaters in the mighty Himalayas, from where it is fed by some of the highest and steepest rivers in the world. The Dudh Khosi is one of these awesome feeders, rising nearly four miles above sea level, on the flanks of Everest, emerging from the icy nose of the mighty Khumbu glacier. To describe it as "extreme white-water" is to cage in inadequate words the scale of this explosive and savage beast of a rock-filled river. The scale of Everest dramatically magnified the extreme danger. Altitude sickness, snow blindness, avalanches, frost bite, leeches and dysentery are not normal parts of a canoeing expedition. They were centre stage in the adventure in 1975, undertaken by Mike Jones and his extraordinary team, who became the first men to canoe down Everest.

They drove nearly 7000 miles from London to Kathmandu in a single, not very reliable, mini-bus, carrying their supplies and kayaks with them. They then trekked a further 180 miles to the top of the river, two thirds of the way up Everest at 18000 feet, with a team of Sherpas to carry their supplies and the boats. On their first hours in the water the river broke six of the kayaks which, in those days, were made of fibre glass, three of them in half so that they could not be repaired. The six paddlers, all of them great men, had spent the day defying death by numerous possible mechanisms of which drowning would have been the most pleasant. Repairs were undertaken and safety plans revisited. They eventually made it a further 50 miles to the bottom of the relentlessly violent waters of the Dudh Khosi and to the wonderfully named Namche Bazaar. It is one of the great achievements in the history of canoeing.

Mike Jones, a doctor and the outstanding young leader of the expedition, died two years later while rescuing a fellow paddler on The Braldu river in the Karakorams, another life tragically claimed in the shadow of the monster mountain that is K2. One of his favourite sayings, which now had the ring of familiarity to it, was: "hypothetical conjecture is just a waste of time, let's Just Do It".

Colonel Blashford-Snell, at the invitation of the Emperor Hailie Selassie of Ethiopia, had been the first to organise a successful descent of 400 miles of the bucking Blue Nile on an inflatable raft, in 1969. According to Mike Jones, an inflatable raft has certain draw backs when confronted by very sharp rocks, crocodiles and bandits firing machine guns. He organised an expedition in 1972, to demonstrate that kayaks were a better way of getting down the Blue Nile. To deter the aggressive crocs the paddlers armed themselves with pistols. Concerned also that they were being stalked by bandits, at night he decided to rope himself to his friend, fellow kayaker Mick Hopkinson, and sleep back to back in a sitting posture, each holding a gun. The bandits were clearly fooled by this deception, but in the morning Hopkinson woke to find Jones's gun with Jones's finger curled round the trigger, pointing into his face. Such are the perils of not having suitable sleeping arrangements during a canoe expedition.

Spate rivers are common in Wales, where steep topography and heavy rainfall combine to deliver big pulses of water down a myriad of valleys. Rivers which are innocuous streams for most of the time can become torrents for a day. While some are too dangerous to canoe, others are great fun, and the country is a Mecca for the sport of white-water kayaking. My brief research of the river we were heading to suggested that The Rhiw was a fairly gentle challenge, with only one grade three plus rapid (Four in some conditions) which, while not really doable in an open canoe, could be portaged round. We were relieved to be heading to this friendly little valley and not to an angry Dee, and our discussions of the Dudh Khosi seemed to have put in our minds that a little river in the Welsh borders could not really be that exciting. Watching television can give a distorted impression of reality, we were soon to discover.

Gundrada had decided to accompany me to our friend's castle, so the journey there was pleasantly devoid of me having to worry about any directions. Or what speed to travel. Or how close to the car in front I could get. Or whether the traffic lights had changed. Or which services to stop at. Or which gear I should use…

We had the canoes on the trailer behind the land rover and eventually arrived at our friend's castle, remarkably, still happily married. John was nowhere to be seen. He had recently switched phone networks and was on a wonderfully cheap deal, so he had boasted. We had been completely out of contact with him for most of the journey. Eschewing a conventional satellite navigation system, he used his telephone for the job. He got very lost just after Shrewsbury, and only instinct and local consultation got him to the castle at all. I was quite used to John disappearing and while we were waiting at the Castle for him I related to Gundrada a story from a bygone Rustic cricket tour.

Not many months after his triplet daughters were born John arrived on the tour, announcing that he needed sleep. This he proceeded to do with energy and he wasted not a single moment by being awake. On the night in question, after quite a long time in a rather remote Devon pub, senior Rustics declared, not unusually, that John was lost. No one had seen him for nearly three hours and the caring Simon, our then Tour manager, suggested we curtail the cricketing party and organised search parties. Simon himself decided to look for John by attaching himself to the outside of a Rustic Land Rover, which was promptly driven through ten foot high stinging nettles beside the narrow Devon lanes. John was not to be found anywhere, though Charlie, one of the younger and least well behaved of the Rustics, claimed to have found a bison.

The following morning, at our camp site, a very dishevelled-looking John appeared for breakfast. He said he had had a good night's sleep in a nearby barn, comfortably curled up in a bale of hay. We re-traced his steps later that morning and discovered the barn in which he had slept. It was the field shelter for the bison which Bad Charlie had claimed to have found, yet whom none of us had believed. John had slept in the bison's manger without harm. We all thought this to be a lovely tale of inter-ungulate co-operation.

Back in Wales and still waiting for John, we had knocked on the door of our friend's castle. Eventually a man appeared, who worked in the extensive gardens, and asked us what we wanted.

"We are friends of Caroline and Mark's and have come to stay the night," ventured Gundrada.

"They are in Sussex with their children," said the man. Sussex, we very well knew, was a six hour drive away.

We were ushered into the great house and given a cup of tea. Gundrada phoned Caroline, who told her that she thought we had meant the next weekend, but to make ourselves at home until she and Mark got back about midnight. We were a long way from home, we had lost John and our supper plans were in disarray. John, luckily, then appeared before Gundrada was able to pin the blame for the unfolding debacle on any-one closer to home.

There was just enough daylight left for us to have a quick explore of the river. The rapid on the Rhiw that we had been advised about was in the village of Berriew. One look was enough for us to agree to portage past it. It was a "frowning" rapid, one which gathered the water from the whole width of the river into a churning maelstrom in the middle. In the centre of the rapid was a four or five foot high water fall, squirting powerfully between some big rocks. In my "How to Canoe" book, "frowning" rapids were described as best to be avoided at all times, and in any case, waterfalls were simply not possible in open canoes. The decision not to go anywhere near it was made there and then. Gundrada was pleased to see John and I make such a sensible choice, but on further inspection upstream of the rapids, our gentle little river looked to have the manners of a runaway pony. A fast, muscular torrent was the overriding impression, a fact indicating that the river was in spate. My stomach churned with a mix of excitement and dread. Gundrada enquired of both of us whether we knew what we were doing, a question to which neither of us gave a decent response.

It had now become dark, so we found a pleasant pub, parked the vehicle and walked to the back door. As we moved through the car park I was nearly reversed into by a car, driven by a guest who was leaving after what must have been a very long lunch and whose little dog barked at me from the safety of the rear shelf. I thought no more of the incident. We entered the pub, greeted the barman and were promised food when the kitchens opened at seven o'clock. John and I looked at one another in amazement, as our history of finding places to eat on January canoe adventures was chequered. We began listing the many places we had failed to eat to Gundrada, who listened in quiet amusement, safe in the knowledge that our meal was secured for seven o'clock. We prepared to order some delicious house specials from a good menu and settled in for a convivial evening until we could go back to the castle at midnight when our friends were due to return home from Sussex.

We then noticed some blue lights flashing through the pub windows, followed by the sound of a siren. It was a busy main road that ran past the pub, so we carried on chatting. The next thing that happened was the appearance through the door of a fireman escorting an elderly couple wrapped in blankets. The gentleman was the same man who had nearly reversed his car into us some ten minutes earlier and who had just hit a car when pulling on to the main road. Luckily, none of the drivers or their passengers had been hurt.

The Jack Russell terrier had been less fortunate. It had been thrown through the open window of the passenger side door and been killed in the impact. This was a bizarrely unlucky accident which had been witnessed by the chef as he arrived for work. He had moved to the bar to get a stiff drink, in floods of tears. In fact, so traumatised was he by the fate of the little dog that he made gracious apologies to us and said he was going to go home. Food was off!

We did eventually feed, in a hotel in Welshpool, and we did eventually see Caroline and Mark, who arrived home earlier than expected. It had been a memorable night. We rose early on Monday morning, like children at Christmas, ready for our river.

Gundrada drove us to the launch point and dropped us with all our gear, insisting we wore helmets. She was returning to the castle for breakfast with Caroline and we reckoned we would cover the eight miles in less than two hours, judging from the pace of the river, and be at the castle for elevenses. She left us and John and I prepared our canoes for the journey.

John produced from his bag a contraption, about the size of a cricket ball, which he strapped to the front of his helmet. "It's a Go-Pro," he said, seeing me looking at him quizzically. "I'm going to film us on the rapids," he added by way of explanation, knowing that I would not have a clue about such technology. Nothing more could be heard above the roar of this little river and we resumed our preparation, lost in the silence of nervous concentration.

John was first to leave, immediately accelerated into the rushing water by the powerful current. I was close behind, my nerves now giving way to a heightened, adrenaline filled focus. After what seemed like one minute, I passed John who was clinging to a tree with no canoe.

"OK, John," I yelled, "I'll get it!" I paddled on until I reached the canoe, swirling in an eddy in a little river bay. I recovered it, and then John appeared from the bank above and we set off again.

After what seemed like only one more minute, I came across John clinging to another tree, and again, no sign of his canoe. I paddled off after his errant boat, and came across yet another tree, this one growing out of the middle of the river. Without Gundrada present to shout right or left, I plumped for straight on. I couldn't say that was a bad decision, for, in truth, events unravelled so quickly that I failed to make any decision at all. I took my first plunge into the Rhiw.

We had travelled about 500 yards in half an hour, with John capsizing a further three times. I suspected John of certain technical deficiencies, so suggested he follow me. In what seemed less than a minute, I slowed to tackle a bumpy section of bucking river and saw John's boat with no one in it pass me and shoot down river. I followed, initially relieved when I saw it pinned to a fallen tree conveniently on the edge of the river. John was out of the water again and on the bank. We got to the canoe at the same time. We pulled my boat from the streaming water and set about rescuing his.

After an hour and a half, fighting in water up to our chests, we had still failed to rescue the canoe. Not surprisingly, as it was a grey January day, we declared ourselves too cold to continue with the boat reclamation. The river was so powerful that we had difficulty standing in water that was only waist deep. I had never seen someone look as cold as John, who was nearly hypothermic. We only had ourselves to blame, but no amount of levering, rope pulleys and grunt from the two of us big strong farmers had any impact. The canoe had begun to distort round the tree and was nearly bent in half. Even rescued, it was a write-off. In The Dudh Khosi expedition the broken canoes were given away to the Sherpas, who used them as herb planters and chicken coops. We hoped our abandoned boat would provide a use to someone lucky enough to salvage her when the waters subsided.

We had covered about half a mile in just over two hours. The only way of getting home was by canoe, so we got some dry gear on, warmed up and got ready to tackle the river once more, this time two in the boat. Before we left, John said we had better have a look at the film he had made on the Go-Pro. The film was a mash of sky interspersed with jerking images of tree branches and green murky underwater blurs. It was clearly an amateur first attempt.

For some reason, re-combining Hole and Dinnis in one canoe proved wonderfully successful. This was a surprise to both of us and we began to enjoy the challenge. The next six miles down to the fringes of Berriew were undertaken without further capsize. We had ridden white water for most of the journey and had developed something of an understanding between ourselves and the river. This was the experience we craved, but which we had in part tried to avoid by coming to this supposedly friendly little river.

The first houses of Berriew sped past and I yelled to John above the roar of the torrent that we had better get out as soon as possible to portage the rapid which lay a short distance ahead. The banks were steep here and no obvious landing place could be seen.

"John, you remember when we looked at the rapid, there was a sort of smoother channel to the right, which didn't go down the waterfall," I yelled. "Do you think we could make it?"

"No!" I heard him reply, very clearly.

Events were moving quickly. We were pitching in very rough water, riding a frothing maniac, soaked by spray, but coping. Landing still looked impossible. The river here had very steep rocky banks and the water was just moving too fast to do anything else but carry on paddling. Suddenly we were in the maw of the great rapid with its waterfall, 20 metres to go, bucking in the rocky stream alarmingly.

"No!" shouted John again, and then some words that I couldn't quite catch.

"Right, paddle right," I screamed as we hit the top of the frowning formation. Right we went, but not hard enough. We hit a rock which sent us left, we were going river centre and over the water fall. In a thrilling moment we shot smoothly over the top of the cascade and dropped into the base of the rapid, paddling like panicked ducks. We then discovered the grim reality of the "frowning rapid." We had gotten down to the base of the tumult and perhaps even had time for a millisecond of exhilarated self-congratulation. Before we could react, the entire river uncoiled itself like a live reptile into our canoe.

About 100 metres below the fall I met up with our canoe, which I pulled ashore. John had taken a long time to surface. He is naturally buoyant and as I have said before, uncommonly like a seal. He drifted down in the water to where I was and quite inexplicably (and inexcusably) announced that he had not been wearing his life vest. A distinctly puzzled frown clouded his face. I grinned at John, relieved to see him, yet I noted that he was not entirely in one piece. By that, I meant he no longer had the Go-Pro on his head, another souvenir of our visit claimed by the Rhiw.

We returned to the castle for a late lunch with our friends. Gundrada had hung about on a bridge after leaving us at the start of our adventure, hoping to see us pass below. She had got cold and bored, and assuming that we were alright had driven back to Sussex. Some rescue crew! I phoned her, like a small boy, and bragged about having a "proper wreck". I assured her that the cataract we had just been over was only about a five foot drop, nowhere near the 186 foot record for canoeing off waterfalls. I discerned a mixed tone of relief and disapproval in her response and, like my mother those many years ago, she muttered something about "Boys will be Boys."

We had planned to canoe a stretch of the River Severn on the following day, from Shrewsbury down to Ironbridge. As already mentioned, we were in a wet winter, and that week The Severn was in the act of coming out of its bed yet again. Several low-lying fields were already under water, and the river was angry, strong and swollen. We followed the river to Ironbridge, where the water flooded through the Gorge and beneath that famous and beautiful bridge. We were awed by the power of the water. It had a steel grey menace that was threatening and violent in its muscularity. We decided we had endured enough adventure for one January trip and made the decision not to get back into the water on this expedition.

John had booked a hotel in the middle of Shrewsbury and used his newly contracted telephone to not guide us to our destination. The trailer carried the one surviving canoe and after an hour and a half of being completely lost in the medieval city centre and having had to reverse out of several narrow cul-de-sacs and one way streets, we eventually abandoned our vehicle in a truck stop. We walked into the city centre. Walking, it took us less than five minutes to find our hotel.

We had a convivial evening, spent mainly in a pub by the river, talking to locals. The pub had won awards for its real ale and the locals told us some depressing tales of drowning in the mighty Severn. One of them said the river was over 70 feet deep through the middle of Shrewsbury. I countered with the fact that the River Congo was nearly 750 foot deep in places, supposedly the deepest river in the world. The locals then recommended a fine Italian restaurant for our supper.

During the meal we were joined by the owner of the restaurant at our table. We were his only customers that night. Conversation ranged from farming and food and back to rivers. He listened to the account of our adventure on the river we were now calling The Rhiw Khosi and, after he left us, we mused on the fate of many of the world's high rivers. In South Island, New Zealand, only 16 rivers have not been dammed for hydro electricity, all of which have current applications for dams. In Nepal, increasing numbers of rivers are being dammed and the same is happening in Tibet, on the Chinese side of the mountains. There are now a group of environmentally-aware canoeists who call themselves

The Last Descents, who set out to paddle these disappearing rivers before the dams rob them of their wilderness. Reflecting on Mike Jones's first descents, the tragic irony that is now being played out over the fate of these precious places was not lost on John and I.

On our return home the following day, we went shopping for a new canoe.

Chapter 11
The Varenne - An Encounter with the Maire - April 2014

John's version of events

Martin and I had been discussing which river we should tackle for this April episode. He wanted to do the upper part of the Severn, but, when I asked him why, his response was that he wanted to see "Powys in the Spring time," punning sickeningly on Paris. Not only did he laugh at his own jokes, but he was liable to repeat them, so The Severn was not viable. It was my turn to choose and, falling back on my French ancestry, I decided we would cross The Channel again

When I organise a canoe trip I try to arrange an adventure that won't cause either embarrassment or inconvenience to other people. In our many outings we have been able to live by this dictum, if only by the narrowest of squeaks. What makes this achievement remarkable is that Martin has been present on all of them and he has the sometimes excruciating ability of putting his foot firmly in "it."

This was to be a two canoe outing, so there was discussion of likely paddlers. I suggested Peter Holborn, who had recently retired. A one-time opening bowler for the Rustics and latterly head of nature conservation at Suffolk County Council, Peter had just celebrated his sixtieth birthday. Peter still comes on the Rustics tour, though he no longer bowls, having lost his run up in a curious case of the "yips." For most of his cricket career he had a long workmanlike and methodical approach to the crease but, as he had neared the age of forty he lost his self-confidence entirely and his run up assumed the course of a wonky and spluttering squib. He never regained his bowling ability, but remains one of the eminent silver-haired members of the "woolly mammoth" brigade.

During a tour in the early 1980s Peter had an attractive girlfriend called Two Star, and he was due to take her away on a romantic break after the cricket. Peter had booked a flight to somewhere special immediately after the last game of the week, which was then played at Blandford Forum. It was a trip designed to win back her heart, after what he described as a run of boyish misbehaviour at which she had expressed a not very vague disapproval.

Blandford were a good side and we were invariably a bit jaded at this stage of the tour. The match in question, 1983 I think, was no different. The Rustics had undergone something of a batting collapse, courtesy of a fiendish Dorset spin bowler. Peter was a poor batsman but still ranted at the team, all of whom batted ahead of him, to "just hit the bloody thing." It was not long before he found himself being called upon to bat, rather earlier than he had wanted. He announced that he would undertake the saving of the fragile Rustic dignity and walked out to the wicket.

He immediately tried to hit the spinner over the pavilion. It was a shot he had never succeeded with before and on this occasion he proved consistent. The ball bounced and span like a Dervish on Red Bull, bamboozling him completely before coming off the edge of his bat and upwards into the middle of his face. The physics was complex, because the ball had been bowled quite slowly and, before meeting his face, had been accelerated through a perfect mix of leverage and percussion. The injury was dramatic, though once he eventually stopped bleeding and regained consciousness, not serious. To add insult to the injury, the cricket ball had simply looped up off his forehead and into the hands of the nearby fielder standing at "short leg." He was out first ball, cold and caught! As a precaution he was taken away to the hospital.

Meanwhile, having lost the match, and while we were drinking in the Blandford pavilion, Two Star arrived. She was dressed for a romantic break, but was not looking very chirpy. There was a plane to catch, very little time, and no sign of Peter. We did our best in his absence, but her humour darkened. The flight dead-line passed before Peter reappeared from A&E, bandaged and displaying two black eyes, looking like a wounded version of Kung Fu Panda. The flight had been missed and, in front of everyone, Peter was summarily told that their relationship was definitely and permanently off. Two Star was not a lady with whom one trifles.

At Peter's 60th party, held more than 30 years later in deepest Suffolk, only a few weeks before our trip, Martin was introduced to Two Star. She was there with her husband, a friend of mine since college days, and now a local Police Commissioner. Martin, of course, remembered her from the Blandford sacking, those many years previously, though she did not know him. Included in the introduction was Two Star's sister. She is eye-catchingly pretty and, rather irritatingly, smiled encouragingly at Martin. He lit up and responded gallantly, but with no forethought, given she was standing beside her formidable sister, with the words "And you must be Five Star!"

Peter declined my invitation to canoe rather curtly, I thought, considering it was Martin who had been so tactless to his friends. I asked Nigel who, as usual, claimed to be too busy but was actually on a yacht on the Mediterranean. I asked George, but he was on holiday in South Africa. Next I had asked my farming friend who milks cows next door to me. His excuse involved nitrogen applications and silage harvesting and a relief milker who had emigrated. I gave up and told Martin we would go with one boat.

Inconveniently he had already invited Will, who Martin claimed had finished working altogether. Will is a good companion, even though he can often appear out of left field with cryptic comments and absurd interruptions. I asked Martin what Will's latest book was about, as he filled his not working time with being an author.

"It is a sort of Enid Blyton "Famous Five" taking on Muslim Fundamentalism," he replied, as if that was a quite normal thing to write about, and then asked if I should phone Gavin. I did this and, to my surprise, discovered he was available for the trip. Marks and Spencer had recently decided to reorganise and he had been "let go" from their logistics team. Gavin is a perpetual over achiever at work and in constant demand, so I thought the decision an odd one. However, when away from the office, his mind enters the "empty box" with alarming speed. This makes for intriguing stories, a recent one of which culminated in him entering the wrong bedroom and jumping in to bed with his mother- in-law. He is a linguist to rival myself and Martin and while skiing in Austria had charmingly ordered "Omelette without eggs." So, it was possible his ex-employer might have a point.

I enquired further about his dismissal. He replied that they were now trying to re-employ him, as sandwiches were starting to appear on lingerie counters and knickers were on the ready-made food aisles. He was pleased about this, as such madness had not happened when he was in charge and he was keen to return. I told him to ask for double the money and give them three days to consider the offer, during which he could come down the Varenne with us. However, his currently redundant mind was in the "empty box" and Marks and Spencer said they would consider the salary but were unhappy for him to take the risk of disappearing down a French river in a canoe at a time of such dire emergency. They were especially concerned when he told them "It will be fine, as I am travelling with two farmers…"

April canoeing is all about recovery from a busy farming period. I had chosen another river in northern France, following on from the success of The Canche a year ago. the Varenne rises in the chalk hills of High Normandy and is one of a trident of rivers that flow into The Arques, the river on which is found the port of Dieppe. The other two parts of the trident are The Bethune and The Eaulne, but The Varenne has the largest catchment area and the fastest rate of flow and was, consequently, our river of choice. Our mission, I had decided, was to canoe from as near the source as possible to the sea at Dieppe.

We all met at Martin's, as he lives only 20 minutes from the Newhaven ferry. Once we gained land in France, the source of the Varenne was less than half an hour from the port. Less than one hour of driving, in total, to get to the top of a French river, confirming my belief that France was easier to access than many parts of England.

We had plenty of time for chatter on the ferry journey, which was just as well, because Gavin asked Martin how his lambing had gone. He had had a good lambing, in perfect weather conditions, he replied and, with Gavin's naive urging, embarked on an explanation of how his sheep flock operated. I knew that this was unlikely to be a short answer and record the following resume.

"The Romney is a fantastic ewe. It is strong, well-wooled, hardy and resistant to diseases such as foot rot and even to the depredations of liver fluke. Its depth of body is indicative of its ability to live from an all-grass diet and its lower lambing percentage is balanced by its ability to survive high stocking rates, to deliver reasonable numbers of lambs per acre, at low cost. The flock book is one of the oldest in the world and the type of sheep can be traced back on the Romney Marshes of Kent for over a thousand years, as can a system of farming that is based on the sheep's character and the ancient lowland pastures on which they grazed."

I had heard all this before, living as I do in Kent and knowing Martin well, but still I felt a pride in one of the great industries of my county. Martin knew he was straying dangerously into "shop" territory, and he glanced at me with a surprised look, as I seldom allowed him space for such a lecture, and he then carried on as he thought that both Will and Gavin were listening attentively.

"In farming we have choices. Many farmers pursue high output from their sheep by using large amounts of protein feed, hybrid ewe breeding and housing them at lambing. Alternatively, there is our approach. We use the abilities of the ewe to thrive on an all grazed grass system, so she feeds herself, and her natural behaviour is encouraged at lambing to enable her to remain outdoors and rear lambs without too much interference from the shepherd. Lambs are fattened solely on the herb rich pastures. The system is organic and natural growth curves generate the best possible flavour and texture to be achieved in the fat lambs sold. Our lamb is fit for the Queen of England!"

Will, an Australian, and Gavin, an intelligent Englishman nodded appreciatively. However, despite more than two hours left on the ferry journey I decided enough was enough and tried to move the conversation on. I failed, and a question and answer session on Martin's Romneys followed. He was in his element and as I knew the costings associated with his flock, I found myself being drawn back in to this contemplation of the great sheep.

Gavin, surreptitiously, had given up listening, and was fiddling with his phone. He was trying to finalise the new deal with M&S, but there was no signal on the boat and I had changed his settings to Arabic, so he was having problems. Will was only listening out of politeness. Martin's enthusiasm remained undimmed, but eventually I could bear it no longer. I knew what to do. I knew it took little to divert his attention.

"How fast do penguins swim?" I asked, addressing the big sheep farmer. Sheep lecture finished with immediate effect. Gavin looked up from his useless phone and made a further, brilliant, diversionary ploy.

"Did you know that the bulls of Pamplona cover the first hundred yards of their run in six seconds?" Poor Martin, now totally re-routed, was reduced to muttering about Usain Bolt and the Andalusian cork forests where the cattle originated. Will smiled at seeing his friend so successfully discombobulated.

The chalk cliffs of Dieppe appeared on the horizon as France hove into view. Will and Gavin ceased their breakaway discussion about religious freedom in the Middle East, and I reflected on the pros and cons of ferry versus car. At least in a car, especially with the singing straps holding the canoes onto the roof and some sort of music, conversation could be kept to subjects enjoyable to all and easily contained by time and distraction, especially if Martin were made to concentrate on driving.

We cleared the docks briskly and went to explore the point where the River Arques met the sea. We found the river, deep behind an abandoned industrial site, and discovered that it joined the sea under the town in a vast complex of subterranean pipes and giant tidal sluices. The Arques simply, and vigorously, disappeared into a cavernous looking tunnel. Our summary of the situation was that the canoes would have to land some way up stream, or else we would face the risk of an ignominious death beneath the concrete of Dieppe. This was significantly reinforced when a man, wearing a light blue boiler suit and having a smoke outside a nearby warehouse, pointed at our canoes, drew his finger across his throat with a sick grimace and pointed at the ominous tunnel. Martin thanked the man for the information, in his best French, of which he was most proud, but the man simply looked puzzled and wandered back to his work.

"I expect he is Ukrainian," said Martin, by way of explanation for the man being unable to understand his French. Gavin smirked, as he spoke an unreasonable version of French but had not understood a word either and Will, being Australian, simply said that he had not realised that Martin was speaking a foreign language at all.

We arrived in Saint Saens with plenty of daylight left in the evening and set about reorganising the accommodation I had booked. I had, quite by accident, managed to book the right number of places, but had organised two rooms on consecutive days rather than on the same night. It had taken a long time, after reaching the starting point of our adventure to locate the first house in which we were staying, during which time Martin had become quite insufferable on the subject of my skills at navigation and my bed arranging ability. Once again I had booked a single bedroom with one large double bed. We now had to book a second B&B, as the first had no spare rooms and Martin then drove Gavin and I to our separate abode, which turned out to be equally difficult to find. Apparently he then got lost again trying to find his way back to Will at the first B&B.

Eventually we re-gathered in the town square beneath a gorgeous Catholic church, which still retained some of the original chalk-work in its walls. Martin mentioned that these blocks were similar to "Clunch", (a word he seemed to enjoy), a hard form of chalk, sometimes with a greenish tinge, quarried from the bottom of the limestone deposition, and therefore older and harder than chalk found near the surface. The Varenne tinkled its merry path down several different streams that flowed freshly through the town, none of them particularly navigable due to shallowness and the lack of clearance under the many little bridges. We explored the pretty streets and myriad streams for a while and decided that tomorrow's journey would have to begin just below the town. After a good meal Gavin and I returned to our "gite", where we were to be confounded by the electric gate. Martin and Will set off on yet another odyssey through the town as they left the square in completely the wrong direction. I reflected that maybe the braiding of The Varenne was the cause of our confusions.

There was some delay the following morning caused by Will and Martin being unable to remember where our B&B was located. They had resorted to the telephone and, as mine was turned off, Gavin got a call which he thought was coming from Damascus. Eventually, we were able to meet up and put the two canoes into The Varenne. Disappointingly, it was little more than a ditch at our chosen start point. It puzzled me that the town seemed to have a mill and water running everywhere through the streets, but it only amounted to this ditch by the time it got to the town limits. It was another beautiful and hot sunny day so, without further ado, we launched.

The reason we were in a little ditch soon became apparent when, after a few hundred metres, a lovely chalk stream joined our ditch from river left. The flowing water was clear and filled with streaming crow's foot and banks of burgeoning starwort which bushed out below the water like a verdant, emerald coral. We here joined The Varenne, the crystal river of our imaginings, and left the town drain.

Martin was in my boat, the canoe I had bought to replace the one lost on the Rhiw, and Will was with Gavin in the second canoe, the original Ojibwe. The Varenne was passing through the middle of the Saint Saens golf course. Several things were beginning to happen all at once. The river surprised us with her sprightly pace and we had the added peril of paddling a river which formed a golf hazard. In addition to this, Martin was not paying attention, either waving at the golfers or pointing to lost golf balls on the river bed. This last was too much for me, so we stopped and I jumped into the river and retrieved 30 or 40 of them, which Martin immediately lobbed onto the golf course, an unexpected bonus for the grateful players. I refilled the boat with even more balls before setting off again. Martin started lobbing the balls at Will and Gavin. In the ensuing fracas I neglected my steering and the canoe tipped over, propelling its hard won cargo and both of its occupants into The Varenne for the first soaking of the day.

Our submergence caused no ill effects, indeed it was rather pleasant as I enjoyed a little swim. The water ran clear and fresh, possessing the myriad virtues of the chalk river and the temperature was very pleasant. The Varenne already looked an excellent choice for our expedition.

For the rest of the morning the river passed through beautiful countryside and our journey was wonderfully restful. So brisk was she that paddling was not energetic and we arrived in good time at the small town of Bellencombre for elevenses. This was the ideal relaxation after the hard work of spring on the farm. We lay stretched in the sun on the bridge parapet, companionably eating what we had bought from the cafe.

I changed canoe partners, giving Gavin a seat with me while Martin set off with Will. They made an interesting boat to watch, as Martin gave instructions for steerage which were studiously ignored by Will. He is Australian and it was his bounden duty to challenge all forms of authority and this led to several trips into the undergrowth for the pair of them as they wiggled down the river. I enjoyed watching their haphazard progress. We followed behind passing through several abandoned mills, a hamlet or two and several small farms characterised by traditional stone-built steddings, before coming to a beautifully restored home on the river bank.

It was an old mill house and its lovingly created gardens spilled down to the river on both banks. The Varenne, as brisk as ever, was being funnelled into a dilapidated mill race, so we had to stop. Our canoes would have to be portaged around the obstruction. Both canoes were stationary and each paddler was clinging on to the branches of a pollarded willow tree as the river sped onward. A dilemma now faced us, as we could not go back up the river, the current being too strong, and we could not advance down it, as the way was blocked. On one side of the river was a very much inhabited private home and, on the other, an immaculately tended flower bed with an intricately planted water garden. There was much discussion between the four of us on how best to proceed, and it was unanimously agreed we should get out on the bank furthest from the house.

Delicately we disembarked, putting our feet gingerly between the plants of the garden and then even more carefully lifting the canoes, each pair then holding their boat above their heads. In this position, with canoes aloft, we were caught by the occupier of the lovely house. We froze, not daring to move, awaiting pleasantries from the householder.

They were not forthcoming. The man before us was about seventy years old, bald and about five foot six tall. He appeared to be in an extreme state of anger. I whispered to Martin for a translation, but it was not necessary. Fury has a universal language and rage a distinctive colour.

The four of us looked down at our eight offending feet, each planted carefully between the exotic flowers of the man's garden, then at the choleric man, then at each other and, lastly, at the canoes beginning to weigh above our heads. Both the indefensible nature of our transgression and the absurdity of our position began to dawn on us. Only Will looked really relaxed, but then he was the most naturally defiant. The rest of us looked like guilty school boys.

After an angry and emotional outpouring from the man we still had not moved, nor uttered. Even Martin, so proud of his French, had not offered any words of mollification. Then the angry man played his trump card.

"Je suis le Maire," he stated loudly, in his choleric hysteria.

This did not have the effect he was seeking, though we remained immobile, canoes still aloft.

"Is that some sort of patsy?" whispered Will through a ventriloquist's clenched jaw.

"No, it means he is a female horse," said Gavin, turning his face from the Mayor before changing his mind. "Actually, I think he said he is a town hall." Empty box clearly engaged.

"Mary is his name," said Martin, also through the side of his mouth.

Disaster beckoned, as I wanted to tell my three idiot companions that the maire was, actually, the mayor, a senior figure in the community with a hot line to the local gendarmerie. I couldn't, however, as the absurdity coupled to the prolonged moments of nervousness gave way to a desire to giggle. I noticed Will's shoulders beginning to heave and some snorting noises emanated from his direction. Not only were we treading on the Mayor's flowers, but we were in grave danger of openly laughing at him. Time seemed to have stopped.

Incredibly, Martin acted first. He called across the river in his dreadfully mangled French, "Monsieur Mary, nous allons faire retour au riviere maintenant et nous aurant desolee." Gavin then started to wheeze and the four of us beat a fast, but orderly, exit from the garden, rapidly redeployed the canoes into the river below the house and made good our escape. Only once we were back on the river did we completely dissolve into fits of childish sniggering.

The river then passed into some peaceful woodland. About half a mile from the incident with the mayor, we came across a tranquil pool. Two fishermen were packing up their fly rods.

"Bonjour," hailed Martin, "Desolee d'etre dans votre fishing, mais nous sommes Allemagne."

"No, you are not German," came the reply, in perfect Oxford English, from the taller, younger one. "You are English, and ought to be somewhere else." He smiled, though, and we cleared the scene amicably, apologising profusely as we sped down the stream, genuinely hoping we had not in any way spoilt their enjoyment of this lovely river. Martin was most surprised that he had not got away with the lie about being German. He commented on the good nature of the young angler whose activity we had interrupted, though he maintained that in France we did actually have a right to travel on the river. He also suggested to me that never, on an adventure that he had organised, had we ever upset anyone, let alone two incidents in less than one mile. Unfortunately for me, he was correct in that assertion. I had been more worried by the maire than the others for a good reason. In a trip to the Paris Show in my student days, I had driven up a one way street. At the end I was stopped by a gendarme, but claimed not to have seen the signs. The gendarme was not amused and pushed a sub machine gun into my back so that my nose pressed against the relevant sign. I re-told this story as we pulled over to the bank a mile or so later, hoping that the maire had not called up his friends in the local police station.

I enjoy swimming, almost whatever the conditions. Martin had recently read an excellent book about swimming in rivers and other natural waters, called *"Waterlog"*, by Roger Deakin, about which he had begun to enthuse. Roger had swum in the River Test, a fabulous chalk river in Hampshire, with some of the best and most revered fly fishing to be found anywhere in the world. At nearly a million pounds a mile for the fishing rights, also some of the most valuable. The author had considerable respect for these anglers, writing about the second oldest fly fishing club in existence, The Houghton Fishing Club. They had celebrated their first centenary at Claridges in London, in 1922, where Lord Buxton congratulated them on a catch of 37045 fish weighing in at 31 and a-half tons, information gleaned from their religiously kept chronicles. These chronicles are full of other information and Martin, with great relish, quoted an excerpt from the 1869 chronicle:

"General Dixon, not satisfied with matutinal ablutions, took a mid-day bath in the open river; but, in the interests of morality, he kept his clothes on. Mrs Flowers took an active part in his rescue. And it is proposed that the Club should present her with a medal, for preserving to his country and the Club so inestimable a life, as also for the merit of landing by far the heaviest object that was ever taken out of the river..."

Having fun, while appreciating the river and its sacred inhabitants, was common to both of our activities. I could see no reason why fishermen and canoeists should not be friends. The tall young fly fisherman, I reckoned, had behaved in an amicable way, given the sudden appearance of our motley flotilla in the middle of his pool of quiet.

Lunch time had come and gone without the required meal and we had travelled a long distance. I mentioned this to Gavin, who was in favour of finding food. Martin and Will were ahead, just out of ear shot, but we saw them bear right at a fork of the river. I had seen a map which showed the Varenne splitting into multiple channels as it descended its valley. This was our first experience of a braided river and the plethora of channels was confusing, even though we assumed they all eventually joined up again.

Gavin and I steered left at the fork and, glancing to our right, noticed two men swimming next to an upturned canoe below a little weir. We paddled past. I vaguely remembered that there should be a village nearby, so we stuck to the right hand channel. Rather wonderfully I was proved right. We found a little cafe in the tiny village where we sat down in the sun for a much needed long lunch, waiting for Martin and Will to turn up, but they failed to appear. We waited a while longer. Normally it is me who has the habit of disappearing, but this time it was Martin. And as for upsetting people, I was at the helm of scandal. Somewhere along this river we had suffered a reversal of character traits. Gavin raised the subject of trying to steer a boat with Will and we both laughed at the thought of Martin and he negotiating tight river bends in the brisk flow of The Varenne. In fact, I thought it would be absolute chaos if the next section of the river was to be full of meanders.

After an hour, with our lunch finished and a second cold beer on the table, I asked Gavin if he thought Will and Martin might have been arrested by the river gendarmes. He thought that would pose a problem, as Martin had the car keys. The afternoon section of the Varenne was particularly full of tightly curling meanders, flowing jauntily through some remote pastoral farms. There was dense and thorny undergrowth along the banks for much of the journey and I thought I detected a number of bends where this vegetation seemed heavily indented, as if a large animal had tried to burrow unsuccessfully through to the bank.

When we eventually found Will and Martin at the Chateau, the cause of these impressions in the river bank vegetation became plain. Both had extensive scratch marks all over their heads and torsos. I laughed inwardly at the thought of Martin's boat responding to Will's "Down under" method of not steering, weaving a poor line through the meanders and the strained relations this might have been causing between the two friends.

They seemed pleased to see Gavin and I. Will had thought it was possible that we were either locked up in a gendarmerie or we had missed the bridge and were on our way to Dieppe. I think they were actually pleased to see us because we had their dry bag, which, being identical, had been mixed up with ours when we had changed canoes earlier in the day. They had been standing in the Chateau conversing with the extremely attractive landlady while still in their wet suits, resembling a pair of bedraggled muskrats.

No rift was apparent between Martin and Will. We were all tired and looking forward to a decent meal, which could not be eaten until we had taken a taxi back to Saint Saens to collect our vehicle. Martin was pleased to see Gavin and I, though he was slightly disappointed that we had not at least been spoken to by a gendarme. He was adamant that I had behaved entirely in character by achieving the impossible feat of getting lost on a river.

He observed that in the story of Three Men in a Boat by Jerome K Jerome, they all got lost in Hampton Court Maze. Even they had not got lost on the actual river. But as he had missed lunch, I happily maintained that on this occasion it was him who had become lost, for once, and not me.

The chateau we stayed in was a grand and elegant building, looking like it belonged to a World War Two film set. It had been occupied by the Gestapo during that war, a reminder that this part of France had suffered much in many conflicts. The owner of the chateau was a charming woman and told us that the great building had come in to her family as the result of a game of chess played by her Grandfather. She could see little or no way of paying for its repair and upkeep. I glanced at Martin, who was nodding vigorously, as I knew he believed all large houses to be proverbial mill stones. There were no other guests, so we had the run of this stately home to ourselves. Will was very impressed that I had organised such a splendid place to stay. Martin merely expressed surprise and muttered something about "monkeys and typewriters and Shakespeare."

Gavin had gone for a stroll in the garden, desperate to return several missed calls on his phone from Marks and Spencer.

During supper, we were hijacked again by the verbally-incontinent Martin talking about nature conservation, though he claimed he was on a special subject. He had a dislike of what he called "Conservation Dogma," and told us of how he had buttonholed a senior Southdowns National Park ranger at the South of England Agricultural Show. Martin was irate that a self-respecting body of naturalists could publish a pamphlet that suggested that chalk grassland, on a per-square metre basis, was as botanically diverse as the Amazon rainforest. He was equally indignant that naturally occurring scrub and woodland should not form part of the downland landscapes.

"The forest is three dimensional, it is a column of life that is brim full. A square metre of chalk turf, while sweet, cannot ever begin to compare," he ranted. The column of life had formed his special subject on the Wye and here it was again. He was in danger of being repetitive, which was not allowed in the rules of special subjects. Fortunately, he moved swiftly on to his main theme, via a proposed punishment of the Park

Authority. Martin had threatened that he would canoe down the River Test in May wearing a jacket with Southdowns Ranger printed across the front and the back. "I think that threat gave the poor man sleepless nights."

Martin then continued his special subject on the trout. Globally there are more than 45 types of trout, not counting hybrids. There was even one called the Apache trout in North America. In Arizona conservationists were at work trying to protect populations of this fish against genetic contamination from the widely introduced Rainbow trout. Gavin wasn't sure he was telling the truth, suggesting that hot deserts had very few trout in them anyway. Will, rather more helpfully, said that the introduction of Brown trout to Australia had been a disaster, as they had completely eaten out native species of fish that were endemic to the southern continent and caused a trashing of the river ecology. Martin returned to the Chronicles of the Houghton Fishing Club, telling Will that "Pikes are worse," and that a six pound pike landed in 1853 and cut open, contained a "one pound pike, a water vole and a live crayfish that swam away merrily when restored to the water."

Gavin enquired as to what weight of fish would be toasted by the current Lord Buxton at the bi-centenary dinner to be celebrated by the Houghton club members in 2022, but before this led to detailed further discussions, I asked Martin "How far does a hedgehog walk at night?" I had had enough of trout.

On the morning of the second day Will and Martin still looked as if they had had an encounter with an angry leopard, and agreed to be the road crew. Martin purported to be suffering from a sudden onset of mild flu and Will claimed that paddling in circles had hurt his back. We emptied our rooms of luggage and Gavin carried both of our overnight bags down the stairs. While I gave our room a last check-over, I found Gavin's toothpaste. I went to the balcony and saw the three paddlers in the car park below, held the tube aloft so Gavin could see what I had in my hand, and shouted "Do you expect me to have to carry this down as well?" Will gave me an odd look, as the tube fell to the gravel, but the other two were used to my humour. Gavin and I decided to complete the journey along the Arques, the stem of the trident of rivers, down to

Dieppe.

We left the river bank and went immediately under the bridge beneath which we had hidden the canoes the night before. As we emerged it seemed that the heavens had opened and we were in a hail storm of tropical intensity. I inspected one of these hail stones and noticed that it was suspiciously similar to a golf ball. Taking cover from even more of them caused us to canoe into a most uncomfortable bramble thicket. It was not thunder we heard, but loud guffaws emanating from Will and Martin. Judging by the rain of projectiles, Will's sore back must have been feeling better and Martin's flu must also have disappeared. Our paddle down to Dieppe thereafter was pleasant and uneventful. A rural calm pervaded and the river was filled with shoals of carp. We crossed at least three small lakes and passed several friendly campsites in the still braiding river.

As the river came in to the back of Dieppe it rather lost its charm, but I was keen to get as close to the sea as possible, to properly complete our journey. This meant an awkward set-in to some steps on the bank, next to the fearful hole, which looked like the entrance to Hades, through which the combined rivers of the Arques disgorged to the harbour. Gavin was slow to read my intentions and when he saw the nearness of the fearful hole let off a stream of rather unpleasant invectives. Once on the steps, he calmed, stating that he would add the journey to his list of near-death experiences.

Gavin wandered off at this point and then returned looking altogether happier. His phone now worked, due to improved signal in the town. It seemed that he had made good progress in his negotiations with Marks and Spencer.

It was yet another fantastic sunny day, what the French call "le grand beau." We celebrated with a superb sea food lunch on the front overlooking the boats. Scallops and Coquilles St Jacques were the local delicacy and arrived on a large platter also containing prawns. I thought of the escaping Houghton crayfish as I scoffed the feast, and hoped that nobody would be looking into my entrails any time soon.

Chapter 12
Quantum Stuff on the Otter - January 2015

Recollection by John

"The eyeball of the European robin is particularly interesting," started Nick.

It was special subject night on the January expedition. Four of us were in the Tumbling Weir Hotel in Ottery St. Mary, in deepest Devon. We were gathered here for our second navigation of the River Otter, this time in two canoes. Hopeful of finding sufficient water in the river, we intended to journey from Honiton to the sea.

Nick was a new-boy on our canoe team and, as he was not a farmer, I assumed he was un-employed. This was indeed the case. In our strangely inter-connected world he played hockey with George for a team called the Blandford Flies, named after the rare insect also known as the Blandford Bomber, which lived along the Dorset Stour. Nick had also been at school with Martin at Eastbourne - although had only met up with him two or three times since. He had been billed as fiercely intelligent, an Oxbridge scientist no less, and a fit and able sportsman. In his current employment gap he had taken up sea kayaking while his equally impressive wife went to London to work. Martin, with whom I had travelled down, seemed excited about seeing him.

"Sounds a bit irritating, him being good at everything," I said to Martin.

"Oh, no, you will like him. He is quite human. He was nearly as pathetic with girls at school as I was," came Martin's retort.

That re-assured me, and Martin was right, I took an instant liking to this shy gifted man. What's more, he was embarking on a special subject rooted in Quantum Biology, a subject I had once brought to the table but which had been rudely under-mined by those snorting fools Gavin, George and Martin and some ridiculous folding napkin. This evening promised to be a great addition to the canon. I hoped George and Martin would behave themselves this time round.

"The robin has an extraordinary ability to navigate accurately, whatever the conditions, which has puzzled scientists for many years," said Nick. "If held captive in a hut with no windows or any other points of reference, they will scratch a way out at exactly the compass point that would be predicted for that season's migration. This is being explained through the application of Quantum scientific theory." He also explained that a rare metal isotope has been discovered in the eye of the robin, and it has free electrons that can "relate to their mirrored twin elsewhere in the universe. A sort of sub-atomic triangulation system dependant on a communication between separated particles."

"If you think you can understand what I have just told you," Nick continued, "then I probably have not explained it correctly."

I looked at Martin, who had briefly sparked at the mention of "twin", yet was looking intensely puzzled. This was the second time he had heard this subject explained in one day as, by sheer co-incidence, I had clumsily been relating the robin's eye study to him in the land rover on our journey earlier in the day. I believe we had got on to the subject when I tried to convince him that Bucklers Hard, an ancient dockyard on the Beaulieu river, by the Solent, in the New Forest, where many of Nelson's ships had been built, was a convenient meeting point. Sipping on his drink, George was grinning proudly, because he had invited Nick and he was proving to be a wonderful addition to the crew.

I was mesmerised, finding this whole branch of science utterly fascinating. The idea of a new dimension to the universe was comforting. I had long suspected that reality was not a simple mono-dimensional passage through the continuity of time. That it was rather more, in fact, and lit by strange occurrences happening in often random ways.

This was our second trip to the Otter. It was the second time in one day that Martin had been subjected to the Robin's Eye. Nick was known by two of us paddlers. Things seemed to be mysteriously happening in pairs and there seemed to be connections within pairs that were super-natural. It even seemed possible that matter could be in two places at once. Given my hectic paternal duties, I thought it would be rather useful if I could harness this power somehow, and learn how to be in two places at once. This trip, though, was to render even this impossibility possible.

Nick continued his lecture. "The particles in the world we observe are only a result of the decoherence of a much bigger pot of quantum soup. We live on the edge of a quantum universe in which a particle can be anywhere and travelling at all possible speeds. That, though, is only the case if formally observed. Otherwise it is an interpretational issue."

Earlier in the evening while visiting a pub in Ottery St Mary, we learnt much about the town from the Landlady. Martin had also observed much about the Landlady by studying the calendar on the wall, in which she posed magnificently with no clothes, but a reasonably modest pair of beer glasses, raising funds for the Ottery bonfire night celebrations. We had all disposed of two pints of the Abbot, named ironically for its inability to inspire spiritual awakening. Later, in the Tumbling Weir Hotel, listening to the lecture, I mused about "another pair," thinking of both the Abbot and the Landlady's two well displayed attributes, then correcting myself. "Another two pairs." Strangely, I was finding Nick's lecture crystal clear to follow.

"When electron pairs are born they are entangled in a stable system, but are not in any fixed position." Nick continued, as if the Abbot had had no alcohol in it at all. He really was the superman that Martin had described. "Nor do they have a particular speed or spin. Actually, they are doing lots of things simultaneously in different places, definitions of which can only be given probability parameters. Once observed, however, their behaviour conforms to classical physical, Newtonian laws." I could tell that Martin was mentally trying to apply this to the behaviour of his twin daughters, although I was struggling with something called the triplet accelerator theory, which Nick had touched on but said was best left to another day.

"In a robin's eye a photon of blue light dislodges the electron pairing, allowing one of the pair to be affected by the earth's magnetic field. The force is tiny, but causes the release of a chemical called cytochrome, which enables the bird's extraordinary sense of direction."

Nick's lecture was over and so were two bottles of red wine. With regard to pairs, this added to the pairs of Abbot that we had consumed. Twinned pair theory was now going blurry. George roused himself from a chair, in which he had slept soundly, to go to the loo. I thought about the miracle of life at the heart of Nick's lecture, my appetite for the trip down the river tomorrow well and truly whetted.

The Otter is an almost wholly naturally functioning river rising at over 900 feet in the Blackdown Hills. Only about 20 miles long, it cuts through spectacular Permian and Triassic sandstone hills on its descent to the Jurassic coast at Budleigh Salterton. It is a shallow but playful river, its catchment is very steep, and during heavy rain it floods violently. It regularly cuts new channels through its flood plain, leaving cut-off meanders and strangely isolated islands of wetland trees and vegetation, as well as delicious undercut cliffs of deep red sandstone. The poet Samuel Taylor Coleridge was born here. He wrote a sonnet to the River Otter, which contains the following description:

> ".....thy marge with willows grey,
>
> And bedded sand that, veined with various dyes
>
> Gleamed through thy bright transparence!...."

On the previous summer trip we had paddled a stretch instead of playing cricket at Exeter, a game neither of us was selected for anymore due to previous misdemeanours. There had been just enough water to canoe, but a bit of bumping and grinding along the shallows occurred as the river was quite low. We hoped for a more exciting journey by choosing it for our present January trip, when, so Martin claimed, the vast store of water held in the great Devon sandstone would have amply replenished the river's flow.

During the summer visit we had checked out The Otter's course before getting the canoe in the water, each of us driving our own vehicle. Martin had a canoe on top of his old Skoda and I had brought the family people carrier, a rather large, black Mercedes. At a junction I had stopped to look left and right, but before being able to pull away had been smashed into by Martin in his Skoda. He had been looking at the river and, without braking, had driven into the back of the Mercedes. Only a small amount of damage was done, although Martin, who would normally find such an incident funny, looked a little pale. Now that I thought back to this incident I got a visceral understanding of what an entangled pair of electrons might look like if enlarged. How had I not realised that canoes were at the epicentre of any understanding of quantum mechanics?

On our summer trip we had felt like explorers discovering a place of rare beauty previously unknown to mankind. The heavens had conspired to rain over the cricket match at Exeter, but we got lucky with July sunshine and warmth, such is the climate of Devon, and had a magical and gloriously mellow trip on the lower section of the river.

There had been only the one error, well two if we count the clash of the Skoda with the Mercedes. We had descended a small rapid through a bridge and then down a small wreck of an old weir. Below this splashing tumble of fun was a sharp bend, which we managed to go round in good order.

"You know," said Martin, "I really think that our competence in handling the canoe has greatly improved." I think he must have started watching one of the picture-winged damselflies that he had been banging on about, for the very next moment, before I could reply to his silly observation, we hit a large, flat rock that instantly turned the boat over. This was the second time in the day that Martin had not been looking where he was going, giving a fine pair of errors, with the quantum probability of more to come.

During the summer paddle we had found the habitat lived in by the beavers, who had successfully re-established themselves on the Otter. Beginning any story with the concept of beavers on The Otter is going to lead to trouble, and we knew things would be messy when we returned to the Rustic camp that evening, after our team's match at Exeter. To prove that there really were beavers on the Otter we took with us one of the many beaver sticks that were marked by this charismatic creature's very distinctive bite pattern. We thought this might reduce the fine pending for leaving the tour for the day. I will leave the "Submission of the Beaver Stick to the Rustic Fine's Committee" story with the summary that it did not go well for us.

Getting back to our January trip, we began our descent at a hamlet near Honiton, called Fenny Bridges. There was the usual bickering with Martin, who was insisting that this was entirely the wrong place to begin. Nick grinned at this exchange, Martin clearly having not changed very much since they were friends at school. George disappeared, but then re-appeared, doing up the smart dry suit trousers he was wearing after relieving himself in preparation for several hours in the canoes before another stop.

My primary concern was that the river would somehow not be as beautiful as I remembered from the summer. I need not have worried, as the landscape was pastoral bliss and the first birds spotted were two kingfishers. The fish that were plentiful during our summer visit, were less obvious, although lots of little riffles in the river and many serpentine bends more than made up for this in keeping us alert.

What was also less obvious was the replenished river flow that Martin had promised as a result of his bragged understanding of ancient sandstones. The water level, which had been low in the summer, was almost as low now. I do know better than to believe Martin when he says anything technical, but here I am again. There was, however, in the region of about six inches more water than was running in July, just enough to give us good passage on the descent, with only limited scraping on the plentiful river gravels. I partnered George, whose light frame helped the draft of my boat, and Martin had set off excitedly with Nick. For January, conditions were mild, with weak sunlight and no wind. We were in for a feast of a journey.

We had expected to have lunch in a lovely rural inn at Tipton St. John, about half way down the river. It was run by an irascible French chef, and a large sign on the door read "No Wellies". Wearing wet-suits, three of us looked to be clad head-to-toe in Wellington boot material, and were as damp and muddy. Only George would have passed muster. I was wetter than the others because when we were getting out of the canoes I had managed to fall in and was totally submerged. It just happened that at the same moment a party of primary school children walked past, and they were able to laugh even more heartily than my companions. Rather embarrassingly, George appeared from behind a tree yet again fiddling with his trousers. The pretty school teacher, who had been very friendly, then quickly ushered the children away.

Consistent with previous trips, a hot lunch on the January adventure was not forthcoming. Fortunately, all was not lost, as opposite the pub was a tiny shop. In the shop was a proportionately tiny Chinese lady, with an enormous smile and a matching carving knife. We crammed into the tiny space, where our shared bodily warmth soon warmed us up, and Lolita, as we christened the tiny Lady (though she must have been well into her seventies) offered us sandwiches, all made with the threatening-looking knife. She could not have been friendlier, though we understood not a word of the hybrid mix of Chinese accent and Devon dialect. Martin's huge frame, stooped and wedged into the miniature shop, was re-positioned by George in a vain hunt for tomatoes. Lolita roared with laughter when told by Martin, with one eyebrow up, that beavers got sick of eating wood and would do anything to steal a sweet tomato, and that Zoologists referred to such behaviour as "beavery thievery."

On emerging from the shop with our super value lunch, I had another Quantum thought. How on earth did four big men fit into a space as small as that shop? I kept my thoughts on enzyme tunnelling to myself, and we all happily got back into the canoes and headed off towards Budleigh and the sea.

We reached the lagoon and salt marshes behind Budleigh beach at last light and pretty much at low tide. The sky was a glowering red, and the river mouth looked completely different to the last time we were here. Then it had been high tide and the river and the sea met at the same level around the point of the pretty shingle spit. This time it was low tide and the river reached the spit and cascaded down the seaward side in a curving channel cut through the large rounded pink pebbles, in a theme park spill way and out among great rocks revealed by the departed sea.

I looked over at the other canoe. Martin and Nick seemed to be stuck in conference. I guessed at what was being said, Martin would be urging Nick to stop before being caught by the sea. Then the unexpected happened. I watched the two of them breast the river mouth in vigorous harmony, and slalom down the cascade on the beach, and then paddle out into the sea. The sea was calm, and both boats succeeded in negotiating this exuberant finale to our day. Eventually we pulled the canoes out of the sea near the land rover, parked in the car park at the other end of the beach. Nick had coaxed his canoe partner to new heights, and we all stood on the beach exhilarated by our day.

We returned to the Tumbling Weir Hotel a happy band, and that evening followed the same pattern as the previous one. The trip to the Landlady and consumption of Abbot ale went very well, but made us late for dinner, to which we had invited Lester, a local farmer and friend from College.

The dining room was noisy, as a Gentleman's Society evening was also going on in the adjacent room, and we were happy and relaxed. The only other people in the hotel were two nice young men sitting together at a corner table conspiring between themselves and, unusually, were not approached by Martin, who is a habitual talker to strangers.

I then delivered my special subject, a true-or-false quiz about beavers. I thought it went rather well, though they all guessed right when told that a beaver, when pursued by a wolf or a dog, would not chew off its own testicles to divert the chasing predator. Equally, but wrongly, none of them believed me when I said that the largest beaver dam ever recorded, in Northern Canada, was visible from space.

We had seen along the river many signs of beaver activity. Some quite large trees had been felled and some patches of willow scrub gnawed to the ground. This was exciting to see as beavers had been extinct in the English countryside for nearly 300 years. Their return would be a red letter day for conservation, and where better than a really wild little river like The Otter.

Martin sits on the Beaver Advisory Committee for England, a panel set up to sift information on this elusive rodent. He informed us that the Department for Environment and Rural Affairs (DEFRA) were due to announce their decision, as to whether the beavers on The Otter would be allowed to stay or would be captured and returned to captivity. Like me, he had a healthy disrespect for institutions. He enthusiastically explained how the people of The Otter valley had led a campaign to allow the beavers to remain, supported by lawyers from the Friends of the Earth.

We went to bed late, in preparation for a long canoe on the Dorset Stour the following day, and were up early the next morning ready to go. However, over breakfast the two nice young men on the corner table of the night before appeared, came to our group and introduced themselves as Tom and Nick, and said, "Would you mind if we join you?"

It transpired that the two nice men were the science team from Channel Four National News, down in The Otter valley covering the story of the beavers. We agreed to help them with their news story, and to spend the morning with them, abandoning the Dorset Stour. When I was about to tell them we had a member of the Beaver Advisory Committee present I felt Martin's elbow in my ribs. "They only want canoe footage and a tourism story," he hissed, imploring me not to reveal his depth of knowledge to the reporters. Well, our plans have always been flexible.

Tom and Nick were seasoned reporters and qualified with science degrees. They knew they would not get film footage of the beavers themselves. I knew, from my somewhat less than perfect understanding of Nick's lecture, that if these animals remained unobserved they would be freely existing in a parallel quantum world where not even gravity could be brought to bear.

We put all our gear on and left the hotel by canoe, heading towards the rendez-vous with the camera crew. On the way downstream, as we passed a TV cameraman, we paddled up and down for his benefit, but eventually realised that this was a rival news team from the BBC. We pushed on to find our half of the pair of camera crews. "Quantum reporting," I began, but I was now sharing a canoe with Martin, and disentangling these two news crews was the mission he insisted on following. He mentioned something about having digested too great a quantity of quantum already.

We met up with our team from Channel Four and they filmed a sequence which appeared on national television that evening, of Martin and I going down a nice little rapid together. Demonstrating both professionalism and determination, they also spliced together an interview, with Tom being paddled by Martin in a canoe. Martin was incapable of answering any question sensibly and point blank refused any comment on beaver tourism, stating how most people he knew would be taking the question "entirely the wrong way." Tom eventually got the responses he wanted, with Martin enthusing about the magic of rivers and the excitement of the beaver's return after a long period of extinction.

After another lunch with Lolita, we packed and left The Otter valley, to return to our homes and families in time to see ourselves on television. I stood with Julie, son George and the triplets in front of the television. When I appeared on the news, I was in two places at the same time. Now that is truly the Quantum Mechanics of canoeing.

Perhaps even more marvellous than that, DEFRA had bowed to the people of the Otter, and the beavers were to be allowed to continue to live wild.

Chapter 13
The Authie - To Berck in a canoe - April 2015

By Martin

By the end of April both John and I declare ourselves exhausted. My own state of utter depletion is caused by the passage of our lambing and calving, and I am effectively worked into the ground. We lamb just under a thousand ewes at Montague, and calve around 80 cows, so the spring workload is enormous. Why John is exhausted, I haven't yet discovered, though I harbour a suspicion. He has a small flock of coloured sheep, which are looked after mainly by Rosie, and a small herd of about 10 cows, which he repeatedly attempts to sell in deals that never quite seem to materialise. He is also an arable farmer and he claims that he is busy with spring cultivations, but this does not seem overly arduous when contemplating the comfort of modern tractors. My own suspicion is confirmed by his mutterings that Julie is as "frisky as a filly." She is younger than he by a considerable margin, tall, dark and attractive, and it seems that after long working days he is not getting a full night of sleep. I didn't wish to give John the opportunity to crow, so accepted companionship in the shared burden of the farming season.

Our previous trips to France had yielded great fun in delightful settings. I knew we had been lucky with these adventures and thought that we could not expect to be as fortunate every time, so had a relatively low expectation. However, I was so exhausted, post lambing, that even the prospect of a quiet descent on a placid, but pretty, little river was very appealing. The equally exhausted John was in full agreement. He had taken charge of arrangements and decided on the River Authie, a gorgeous chalk river rising on the extensive plateau of the Pas de Calais, and flowing some 100 km from its source to the sea just north of the Somme. Running parallel to, but south of, the Canche, it flows through lovely countryside and small villages graced by some beautiful old fortified farmhouses, chateaux and abbeys, elegant country surprising in the sometimes bland and industrial landscape of this part of northern France. Its egress to the English Channel is through the spectacular estuary of the Baie d'Authie, famous for its wildlife, vast expanses of sand, ferocious tides and the winds of Berck, an old fishing port and holiday resort at the mouth of the bay. Despite these wonderful ingredients in our proposed journey, what John and I craved most were a couple of long nights of deep sleep. Our chatter prior to leaving home had been muted and unimaginatively centred on how to "get two berks to Berck and berck home again."

In this torpid state of mind we met at our friend Nigel's house, as we had before, on our journey to The Canche, two years previously. The two robotic mowers had procreated and turned into four. To keep these strange automatons busy, the gardens had been enlarged, to create another acre of lawn. Appallingly, I saw, in the middle of the extended grass, a life-sized, steel cut-out of a bull. Our normal sense of mischief was muted by tiredness, but thwarted entirely when we discovered that Nigel was not at home, and had left the house guarded by a muscular-looking house-keeper. Nigel was watching cricket in the West Indies, having yet again said that he was "too busy" when we had suggested he accompany us on our expedition. John left his zebra-striped land rover parked in the drive and transferred his kit to mine. We then departed from Nigel's to catch the ferry to France.

I had altered the method by which I attached the canoe to the roof rack, largely so that I did not have to get tangled up with the ratchet straps, my operation of which gave John much ammunition for taking the mickey. The unforeseen benefit of this was that we could hear each other speak in the car, as there was no longer an infernal drumming noise. We were both very fond of Nigel, believing him to have the incorruptible soul of a fellow peasant, but the mechanisation of his lawns and the appearance of the cut-out tin statue of a black bull were disturbing. I was fond of teasing Nigel about being simply an "arable famer," which, coming from a sheep and beef man like myself, was really a dig at the stereotype of the environmental banditry of a "grain baron." I sent Nigel a text enquiring about the tin bull in rather impolite terms. The Test match must have been dull, or finished early, as I received an immediate response, as follows:

"Everybody apart from you admires Angie's bull. It does not require feeding, remains on the right side of the fence, does not become ill, needs neither ear tags nor movement records and is not exchequer negative. I also own exchequer negative living cattle, and maintain that any comparison with Milton Keynes is libellous and intellectually unsound...I have instructed my Brief. I hope you are insured!"

I showed John the message from our friend, and we were both happy to have stirred the old Mammoth, though a little concerned that we had mocked Angie, Nigel's adorable wife, by mistake. I sent a text back to Angie, by way of apology, suggesting that;

"Were the tin bull actually a tin cow, there would be an opportunity to not produce tinned milk, and the cow could be not fed by importing alfalfa not produced by the farmers descended from Major Major's father," (thus recalling the great passage from John's beloved *Catch 22)*.

I think Angie, from New Zealand where they no longer subsidise farming, was puzzled by the multiple negatives, as this text was not answered. John later commented to me that the message did rather resemble a policy guidance note from DEFRA.

Nigel's brief, a left arm spin bowler called Paddy, was also a good friend of mine. I had ushered at two of his weddings and prior to the first of those, had been party to an "incident" involving the Counter Terrorism Unit of the Metropolitan Police and some Irish bagpipes in Highgate Cemetery. I had also once shared a near-fatal meal of "Doctor" fish under some giant baobab trees on the West Coast of Africa, during a cricket tour with him. With such shared adventures, I felt sure that Nigel's choice of advocate was liable to be counter-productive to his cause.

In the quiet of the car I continued with my fulminations, selectively quoting from the great oration of Charlie Chaplin, pinched from *"The War of the Worlds,"* that "we are not machine men with machine minds and machine hearts."

"You definitely aren't, because you are a livestock farmer," John replied, "and you know full well that means you have no affinity with machinery."

John is mainly an arable farmer, and finds my mechanical ineptitude amusing. On a Dinnis family visit to Montague, I had proudly shown John and his son George a very expensive bit of kit that I had bought to electronically weigh, sort and identify my ewes. We got some sheep into the pens to demonstrate the "Way Forward" for sheep farming, but I was unable to locate the 'ON' button or get the tag reader to work. The thirteen year-old George, who had never seen such equipment before, pushed me out the way and got the whole thing running. I hadn't yet admitted to John that I was still unable to get it to read a tag, two years later, though the automated weighing and shedding was proving a success.

"You could never live in Milton Keynes," said John, sympathetically. "The concrete cows would turn you madder." The conversation turned to the values of the Maasai Elders in the Rift Valley of Kenya, and their love of real cattle, before we arrived at the ferry terminal in Dover, and joined a queue of vehicles.

While queuing, John told me a story. He had taken his family and some friends to Holland in Acorn, his 54 seat bus. Under the rules of the ticketing office, carrying ten people qualified the bus as a commercial vehicle, but if there were only nine the cost would be much less than half. As Julie was the only person qualified to drive it, John said he would go by foot and so gain a cheaper bill for crossing the channel. Apparently, he had then wandered off on his own and got on to what he thought was the right ferry and once on board had been unable to find either Julie or the family. He phoned Julie, who instructed him, sternly, to go to the rear of the boat, which had just unmoored and was moving away from the quayside. There, he was instructed to look down and back toward the docks, and to wave at his children who were all looking up at him as he sailed away from them. He assured me that this experience had taught him to be very careful with ferry bookings.

As we checked in with our ticket I was asked how tall I thought the vehicle was, including the boat on top. My new roof rack system involved four padded uprights, forming a cradle for the canoe. It appeared that the height of the uprights was about to invalidate the ticket and we had become too tall to be a car any more. Using the sort of stick used to estimate the height of a horse, the vehicle was duly measured. We would need an alteration to our ticket and would have to go into the deck with the 120 articulated-lorries which also used the ferry. Our objective was to make the two o'clock sailing, but the nice girl in the office said our earliest guaranteed slot would be eight o'clock, unless we were lucky.

We went into the giant car park of the ferry terminal and I berated John for his inept organisation.

"Surely you knew that a car with a canoe on its roof is taller than one without," I remonstrated hissily.

"Stop fretting," he retorted. "I have a plan." He then wandered off into the depths of the quayside industrial structures. He disappeared for a while, which I was well used to, and I dozed off in the warmth of an uncharacteristically hot and sunny April afternoon. After some time, he re-appeared, looking exceptionally relaxed. "I've sorted it," he said. "I've told the loading officer that you are educationally sub-normal and that I am your carer, so please could he ensure that we get on to the two o'clock boat, or else the boredom might bring on a fit."

We were duly waved on to the back of the ship, for the two o'clock sailing, and parked behind the huge lorries. As we passed the loading officer he gave us both a very strange look. However, at least we were on the right ferry and heading to Dunkirk and The Authie. After the debacle with the ticket, I didn't like to ask John why he had booked a ferry to Dunkirk, but I did anyway. His answer included the facts I already knew, that Calais would have been 40 minutes nearer to our destination and a 40 minutes shorter ferry journey. To have taken the Calais ferry would have shortened the trip by an hour and twenty minutes. The bit about straight lines and triangles was hard to understand and we both agreed that maybe tiredness had clouded his judgement. His natural inclination to deviate had asserted itself once again.

We gained our first sight of the river that evening, having arrived at our bed and breakfast in Auxi-en-chateau. This small town was about ten miles from the springs at the source of The Authie, but already it was a river of a brisk and healthily muscular character. Above the bridge in the town centre we could see white water and, beneath where we stood, the river current swirled and eddied swiftly as it poured its way downstream. It looked exuberant and fresh, pristine as fisher-folk are apt to say, all things that did not currently apply to the exhausted pairing of John and myself.

That night we were cooked supper by our hosts, each of them retired police officers from England, and went to bed early. Our hostess had kindly agreed to help us with the logistics of getting our car to the next hotel, down the river at a village called Argoules. In the morning, after an early breakfast, and while John went back to sleep in the canoe, we deployed the vehicles as required. At about nine o'clock I was able to re-awake John and we got onto the river and away.

It was a dreamy spring morning, with a dewy mist that was rapidly dispersed by the rising sun. We quickly decided that the river was even more beautiful than the Canche or the Varenne. The speed of flow was a relief as the day's journey was about twenty five miles. Roughly eight hours of paddling, we reckoned, so long as nothing dramatic occurred. Our first obstacle of the day was the white water above the bridge and we negotiated that very easily. Filled with confidence we passed out of Auxi and into the countryside of this pretty valley.

The first bird of the river that we saw was a common sandpiper. My mind, still suffering the chronic grip of fatigue, groped for the Latin name of this little wader, but could only generate the first bit. "Actitis," I said, hesitantly, and then I received a flash of inspiration from something silly I had once read about this charming bird. "Actitis dinissiae, or, according to a tribe in New Guinea, the "Matakakoni," which means the bird that walks like he copulates," I continued. Our little wader has a gait, when on the ground, full of busy tail pumping and head thrusting, that British ornithologists refer to as a sewing-machine action. I looked back at John over my shoulder, as he was steering the canoe. I had been casting several aspersions at him concerning my theory as to the real cause of his tiredness. This little bird was a heaven-sent opportunity to continue in that vein. He smiled wanly, not really enjoying this little verbal ambush, only saying to me how fresh the sandpiper looked in its subtle spring plumage.

Above our inane banter the note of the river had changed. Its quiet babble was replaced with a roaring noise. Ahead I saw the remains of a derelict water mill and a broken sluice that crossed the river. There was a choice of four gaps to aim at in the sluice and had we chosen either of the two in the middle, or the one on the right, we would have ridden the race of churning water easily. However, I was feeling over relaxed as a result of still being tired. My mind was still enjoying getting one up on John with the Actitis dinissiae. He later simply admitted to being too exhausted to either react or make a decision, so it was through the left hand gate we went, travelling rapidly.

The force of the disrupted river banged us into some old brickwork partially submerged beneath the flowing torrent and the collision turned the canoe over. The suddenness of our capsize was quite violent. We quickly discovered that though the day was warm and sunny, the water was freezing and the muscular vigour of The Authie very evident. We were both out of our depth in the swirling river below the weir, so had to save ourselves before returning to rescue the boat and our paddles and dry bags.

We eventually lugged everything on to the river bank, emptied the canoe of water, and took stock of our surroundings. The river sides were well wooded, in places with the perennial poplar plantations, with their bouquets of mistletoe, but interspersed with more natural trees, predominantly alder. The whole valley had an air of deep countryside about it, with even a touch of wildness. It was a pleasing palette of farming and trees and wildlife. Just along the bank from where we were re-organising ourselves there was a notice board. It had colourful pictures of birds and plants on it, and the heading of "Le Marais D'Authie." At the bottom of the sign, which had an English translation on one side, were the instructions: "In order to protect wildlife do not go swimming and do not dive into the river voluntarily." We had never before seen such advice and particularly liked this use of the word "voluntarily." It was already too late for us to comply. Laughing at the sign, we got on with our journey, as we had a long way to go and had not yet completed our first hour.

I decided, lethargically, to continue my lecture on the common sandpiper, as they were plentiful, feeding on the river edge and flying with stiffly-arched wings along the river in front of us, skimming no more than a millimetre or two above the surface of the water. I told John that I had once seen one of these little chaps picking ticks off the eyebrows of a hippopotamus, in the Kassinga Channel in western Uganda. As I waffled on, I saw a little grebe duck down under the river. "Tachybaptus ruficollis," I blurted, "carries its young on its back, and then submerges like a submarine. In fact the sandpiper is supposed to be able to carry its young on its back when flying as well. What a coincidence! Submerging like a submarine! That's sort of what we have been doing." John, I could tell was losing interest. "The little grebe has extraordinary but highly effective lobed feet." I decided to finish there, as my own words were beginning to make my eyelids heavy. I had bored myself.

We paddled on, enjoying the fresh briskness of the river. The valley floor, as is often the case, contained good grass growing land and for several miles we were passing through well organised dairy farms. Many of their young stock were to be seen grazing on the water's edge. The black and white cattle took a keen interest in the men in the canoe, even if those men had lost interest in themselves, and frolicked playfully along the banks. John then got his camera out and demanded a stop to get some photos of the cattle. The modern dairy cow is carefully bred for production purposes, and these were young Holsteins, with intelligent faces and much personality, but very angular bodies. He took some photos, and commented sadly that their mothers would be stuck in a shed for most of the summer, where their diet could be augmented sufficiently for them to deliver their vast yield of milk. The food required for a cow to produce ten tons of milk, or more, in a single lactation could not come from pasture-fed grass alone. I looked at John, and wordlessly agreed with the sympathy he showed for the plight of the dairy cow.

It felt like lunch time, and as John had all the gadgets for determining our whereabouts, including a map, I asked him where he thought we were. He clearly did not know, but suggested we ought to get out of the canoe and inspect the river ahead. The river was squeezing through a bridge and then straight into a mill race before a large weir. The waters were accelerating alarmingly, and had gathered into large waves of white water. I was steering, and replied that getting out would now be impossible, and why had he not alerted me sooner. I was awake for the first time on our morning's journey, but better late than never, I would argue later. We kept our balance and took an excellent line through the rapidly appearing obstacles. The last of the series was a plunging drop down a seething weir, and we made it, despite the canoe pitching at rather a steep angle.

"Stop mucking about, Dinnis," I yelled over the noise of the water, as we wallowed in the pool below the weir.

"I'm not," he yelled back.

The canoe was tipping from side to side, and John was leaning back on the thwart, not paddling. It looked like he was deliberately rocking the boat. He wasn't, but the half ton of water we had shipped at the base of the weir certainly was, and we sank ignominiously before reaching the bank. My shirt, which had been drying on the spare seat since the mornings earlier capsize, floated away downstream, but we were too busy rescuing all the other gear for it to be retrieved. I thought, wrongly, that it would snag on a tree and we would pick it up when we resumed our journey. I was never to see it again.

All our other belongings, including the boat, were gathered safely on the bank. We took a look around. We were in a garden, overlooked by a grandly converted old mill. To get out we had to climb over an eight foot high gate which, we discovered on the road-side, had "Prive" written on it in big red letters. We hoped the owners had not seen us.

What happened next was truly remarkable. Directly across the road from the gate was a restaurant, and it was busily serving lunch. John noted that it was exactly one o'clock. I pinched myself to see if I was actually awake. This had never happened to us before on our expeditions. Restaurants and pubs were either shut, inconveniently located miles from the river or we were too hurried to visit. John's mouth was open in an expression of bewilderment, and he failed to utter even an "aaah." The pair of us were like two lost men in the desert confronted with a mirage. We had not even realised we were in a village, as the river had been absorbing our attention. And here before us, to our complete surprise, was a lunch fit for a king.

Our hostess took one look at the two men before her, bedraggled in sodden wetsuits, and gave us the only outside table, before offering us a delicious steak in pepper sauce. The dream was real. We sat for our lunch, happily, in the hot sunshine.

As we munched our delectable meal, I said to John: "If only you had kept your mouth shut, you know, I might have believed that you had actually planned this."

"I didn't say anything," he retorted.

"No, you didn't," I laughed, "but your lower jaw nearly hit the pavement when you saw the restaurant!"

"Aaaaah," he sighed, finally managing the noise he reserved for moments of satisfaction.

Lunch was eaten quickly so that we could get back to our canoe, there still being a long journey before reaching Argoules. Re-entering the garden proved tricky, as we were incapable of climbing the steel security gate, and the walls either side were protected with barbed wire. In the end we walked upstream, climbed into the river, and waded down The Authie to the garden where we had left our belongings. Fortunately the owners of the mill had not seen the boat on their lawn, nor the two men with it, and we quickly launched for the second half of the day's journey.

After an hour or so of paddling, and a couple of portages round large, ancient mills, we stopped by a field containing some Charolais cattle. I was wearing a bright-orange cagoule and lay on the grass by the water. I rested with my eyes closed, enjoying a stretch of my tiring muscles in the spring sunshine. There was a rustling noise and the ground started to tremble. It had been all too much for the cows to ignore. Having watched us warily from afar, they now gave in to their curiosity and were coming over to see us.

The creamy white Charolais are one of the largest beef breeds in the world. In England one such Charolais bull weighed in at over two tons, was over seven foot tall, and, harnessed for AI, sired more than 150 calves in a year. Even John could not match that. These cattle are quite simply magnificent. We were in the fertile heartland of the breed.

The cattle that came to the riverside to inspect us were enormous, but docile.   Each of the animals shone with rude health. They were beautifully muscled and regal in bearing. Our own beef herd is nothing like these animals. We improve our small native Angus and Sussex breeds by judicious use of continental blood. Our cattle are much smaller and bred to be easier to care for and cheaper to feed. John had Sussex cattle also, and his father and uncle had been leading lights in the Sussex Breed Society, winning awards and pioneering exports of those hardy cattle to Africa. Our knowledge of cattle, though, enabled us to be awed by the mighty beasts that were now milling round us.

I have a saying, picked up once when selling some sheep in Wiltshire for an unexpectedly high price, that "there is nothing as daft as a farmer with grass." John had just sold his calves as store cattle to another farmer, who would then sell them in the autumn for the same money he had paid John. John thought this illustrated my point precisely. He was fond of describing the madness of beef cattle economics with the apocryphal tale of the man seeking advice on how to make a million pounds from farming. "Start with two," is the answer from the sage.

We once again paddled on our way. John had arranged a very long journey. We had started it tired and now were becoming more so. The Authie meandered with increasingly long bends through darkening alder woods, but it remained vigorous in its flow. Our spirits were kept up by the warm weather, lovely countryside and some spectacular buildings in the rural hamlets. Eventually we came to the bridge by the hotel that was that night's destination, again much to John's surprise, but to both of our relief.

After half an hour's canoeing on the following day, John asked, "Are you sure we are in the right river?"

"No, but then you have organised the trip," I replied, helpfully reminding him that the hotel we had stayed in the night before, specifically for its food, had closed the restaurant. It was another entry to add to the list of organisational haphazardness that had drifted enigmatically yet occasionally fortuitously through our adventure so far.

"Well, my plan was to get from Argoules to either Fort Mahon or Groffliers, before we get sucked out into the Baie, and we have only driven a couple of miles along the valley from Argoules to launch, so we must be in The Authie," he said, trying, mostly, to convince himself.

In order to reduce the day's length of journey I had suggested cutting out a three mile section, as we had a ferry to catch that evening, so we had driven towards the sea and parked the car on the road bridge at the village of Nampont. Fortunately, the river we put into was a tributary of the Authie and after half an hour of paddling we joined the main river. It was like being reunited with an old friend.

After the previous day's trip I had thought that I would be feeling a little weary. But, not a bit of it, I was feeling as fresh and vigorous as the river we were on. We were spoilt with the weather, yet again feeling the warmth of the sun on our backs. On top of that we had started our journey with plenty of time up to spare. The keys to success for the day ahead were to make sure we did not get swept into the estuary and that we beat the incoming tide, which, John had told me, turned at half past two.

The river had changed markedly from our journey of yesterday. We were cutting through the coastal plain, across a flat landscape with diminishing numbers of trees. The last hill we had seen was being grazed by a herd of the mighty Charolais cattle, whose size somehow distorted the scale of the landscape, dwarfing its features. Even the trees looked stunted, out of normal proportions to these mighty beasts. The river banks began to reveal areas of bare mud, a sign of regular tidal movement, but we were happily and briskly running down the river on the strong current of the ebb tide. If high tide was at half past two, this should not be the case, we reckoned, as the water should be filling, not emptying the river. I was puzzled, so I asked John how far it was to our destination. Predictably, he had absolutely no idea.

We grew more puzzled as the landscape of the river became that of an estuary. The river channel became fringed with salt marsh and ahead of us the land opened out into vast expanses of sand and mud flat. The depth of the river was less than a foot. The water wound into an infinite distance. We could stand in the channel and see the shoreline was about a mile behind us. We were heading in the other direction, to a vast flat horizon where water and salt marsh merged with sky.

Amongst a herd of some 50 mute swans lay a seal, who watched us nonchalantly, and everywhere were flocks of waders. Greenshank in small parties, green sandpipers, sanderlings, redshank and avocets all abounded. They were feeding on their migration to northern breeding grounds. The shoreline, still visible far behind us, was formed of mountainous sand dunes clothed in patchy pine forest, part of the Marquenterre Park Ornithologique, and so we reckoned ourselves to be several miles from the nearest human being. Logic, but not organisation, put us firmly in the middle of the Baie d'Authie. It was spectacular. We agreed that it was possibly one of the most dramatic locations we had ever canoed. However, our journey had been organised by John so that we would go nowhere near the Baie. Therein lay the problem.

"Why are we here?" I asked John. Earlier in the day he had asked me if I thought there was life elsewhere in the universe, to which I had answered an unimaginative "No," and I saw him gather himself for a philosophical discussion. That was not what I was after, so I asked if he would consult one of the gadgets he had in his sack. We had beached the canoe on a long bank of sand. I saw John's brow furrow as he peered at his screen.

"We seem to have missed both villages and are now dead centre in the Baie d'Authie. Have a look." I did, and the map device showed John to be correct as did the panoramic view we had of this incredible place. This was not the hell of treacherous tide and relentless wind that I had expected of the Baie, but an extraordinary paradise of eternal wilderness, wet and wind sculpted nature. We both admitted to a feeling of exhilaration.

"We are about three miles from Berck," he said, and the map suggested that if we carried on paddling in the channel of the river we would reach the town. We carried on, still mystified that the tide in the estuary appeared to be completely out, when the level should have been approaching the top of high tide. After a while we could see a cloud of colourful kites fluttering over some high-rise buildings. We knew for sure that was Berck, as it was hosting an international kite flying competition. The town came slowly into view and we started to feel quite pleased with ourselves.

I am not a knowledgeable historian, but this part of France is redolent with the names of horrifying battles, stretching back through the World Wars to medieval times. When Henry VIII unsuccessfully laid siege to Montreuil in 1544, the English soldiers sacked Berck, stealing as much as they could and murdering whomever came into their clutches. The relieving French army then came and did the same, laying to waste much of what remained of the town. I couldn't help feel a little sorry for the ancient burgers of Berck, beset not just by the Atlantic tides, but also by the tides of war.

The land alongside the canoe had been speeding along nicely. All of a sudden it stopped and just as quickly started to go backwards. The wind had risen, gusting strongly, sufficient that we removed our hats and creased our eyes to keep out the blowing sand. The boat caught the gale and could not be properly steered. In every direction there was movement and rapid change, as the long awaited tide began its turn. In a very few minutes the channel we were in completely disappeared, replaced by a hurrying and roughening sea. We were perhaps a couple of miles from Berck, but half a mile or so from a sandy promontory. It was impossible to paddle in any direction, except, possibly, backwards, so we hopped out of the canoe and, towing it behind us on a long rope, headed to the nearest point of the shore. The tide kept pace with us. Towing the canoe was easy, for it remained afloat as the silts and sands behind us were becoming water quicker than we could walk. Luckily, we were on firm sand, so the walk was safe from the threat of perilous sinking sediments. During our nervous retreat, the sea swirled at our feet, rising at a speed that was disorientating and discomfiting.

What was also rather puzzling was that on the sandy shore which we were retreating towards, which I had previously observed to be wild and deserted, strolled an elderly woman with a parasol and what looked to be her six year old grand-daughter. They also had a little dog with them, completing an image of gentle serenity, such as would have been captured in paintings by the artists of Picardy. This was in stark contrast to our predicament. John used the aparition to claim that I was panicking unnecessarily, though there was no diminution in the pace at which he joined me in our escape from the in-rushing ocean.

The wind blew ever stronger and the Baie was filled with sea within twenty minutes of our first noticing the in-coming tide. The scene had become the description of the bay that I had originally feared, a wind-whipped cataclysmic morass of swelling choppy water. The land had disappeared. We looked at the current along the shoreline on which we stood and noticed sand, crumbling from the edge of the dunes, being carried in the water against the movement of tide, directly towards Berck.

The off shore wind and the shape of the bay had combined to cause some sort of circulatory eddy, that could take us the last mile or so to the town in the canoe, opposite to the general direction of the terrifying tidal currents.

We had a test run and, indeed, the water was carrying us on exactly the course we wanted, so we continued paddling. I insisted on staying very close to the beach, as our canoe was not a sea going craft, nor was the sea our friend.

We passed a little island of rocks and Berck approached rapidly. Our moments of fear were diminishing as the scale of our journey reduced. John even wanted to paddle out to see the seals, who were regularly popping their heads out of the water to watch us. I remained steadfast in hugging the shoreline, though John remained manically keen to get closer to the seals. Like the mythical Sirens, they seemed to have intoxicated him with a dose of fatal attraction. The power of what we were witnessing around us was so vast that I refused to give in to John's mad longings.

Eventually we beached the canoe beneath the tip of the Berck promenade, at a sailing club where there was also a lighthouse and a sea rescue service. Our epic journey was over. However, our adventure was about to grow more bizarre. John and I had identical red life vests and, wearing wet suits and standing next to the rescue service building, we clearly looked like lifeboat men. A near hysterical lady came running up to us, explaining in a mixture of French and German that her yacht's mast had snapped in the wind and that the yacht, which she had jumped off but on which her husband remained, was being blown out to sea. Could we help? There followed a fantastic mangle of translation which did, eventually, result in a rescue boat being launched to save her yacht (and her husband). We quietly slipped away from the scene before the proper rescue men could enquire as to how we had arrived. We didn't fancy the sort of lecture that might have been forthcoming.

Chapter 14

A drysuit on the Dee   November 2015

Martin

At one stage John and I were to be joined on this adventure by four other farmers. The six men would have been enough to fill our two boats and a third canoe provided by Toby, a potato farmer from Norfolk. The prospect of this flotilla caused me an element of concern, as the Scottish Dee in November could be a spicy run, and only John and I had any real whitewater experience.

I then received a text stating that "the potato harvest was taking longer than expected." This ruled out Norfolk Toby and the third canoe, reducing us to five men and two boats. My organisation was going swimmingly.

Before long, again without my input, the awkward equation righted itself. "I never intended coming anyway," Tim, a Shropshire cattle man announced when pressed. Six had become four, the correct allocation of men to the available boats.

The week before we were due to leave our homes in Sussex and Kent, we were accidentally copied in to confidential e-mails supposed to pass only between the two remaining Scottish farmers:

"Our shepherd, who's a bit of an iron man, has done the trip in the summer and says we'd be nuts to do it at this time of year," read one of Ayrshire Charlie's missives, directed to his friend Boothie, who farmed near Aberdeen, the ultimate destination of our adventure.

"Our crop-walker has also done it. In July. Says the same," came Boothie's reply. "Our chef in the farm shop says make sure you take a guide who is good at first-aid."

"Martin can be a bit potty and apparently his mate's as bad," was a comment from Charlie a week or so later. (He must have received this solid information on John through the farming grape vine, though I thought it a slightly harsh assessment of myself).

"My wife says we could die," responded Boothie' e-mail. "Let's make our excuses."

Hence, the week before leaving the South Coast, I received a formal withdrawal from my two Scots friends, Charlie politely citing the need to attend a court case and Boothie claiming a sudden need to attend to his wife following an incident on the staircase of their new house. Neither of them seemed to realise that at the base of each of their notes was appended the whole of their correspondence on the adventure. The river would, thus, be run in one canoe, with just John and I making up the team. We were familiar with this type of team-building outcome after various attempts to get men to join us on other escapades.

The upper part of the Dee is arguably one of the most beautiful of all the Scottish rivers. Emerging among pools known as the Wells of Dee, but more correctly called the black tarn of the Lairig, 4000 feet up in the Cairngorms, the young river cascades off the plateau of Braeriach, beneath Lurcher's Crag and over a cliff at the Falls of Dee. It passes the mighty Ben Macdui, the second highest mountain in Britain, 114 feet shorter than Ben Nevis, and other giant "Munros" as it tumbles impishly, like a lithe faun, through the great granite scenery of the Highlands. It descends the glaciated glen to the pretty village of Braemar, where, joined by the jollity of Clunie water, it widens and pours through the heart of ancient Caledonian forest and the Royal Balmoral estate.

John had recently told me that he thought I was ageing rather rapidly, referring pointedly to the most recent Rustic cricket tour where my performances had been besmirched by particularly poor fielding. The triplets combined in the teasing, yanking at my greying side burns whenever possible. I thus took pleasure in telling him that the head of the Dee was the home of the only known British Yeti. In Scotland it was known as Am Fear Liath Mor, the big grey man of Ben Macdui. John thought this to be more than just a coincidence, suggesting the population of "big grey men" in the area was about to double. John's hair had remained annoyingly full and dark; he was not one of life's worriers, so I could not retort with "treble".

The Dee is a twelve hour, 580 mile drive from my home in Sussex. We had decided to take the canoe because I was able to combine the voyage with a farming study tour of Aberdeenshire in a reunion of farmers who had all attended the farm management refresher course at Wye College in 2004, the same that my friend NBF had also attended. John had attended a similar course to this, ten years earlier in his career, but was not part of this reunion. As an idle arable farmer he was simply happy to grab the opportunity for an adventure and would fly home after doing the river, before my old contemporaries gathered. Thus, with the canoe strapped tightly to the roof of the Land Rover, I drove via his house (in Kent) to Leeds, where we would stay the sunday night with our Rustic friend Sam and his family, breaking our journey North into two manageable portions.

Sam was known among the Rustic cricketers, affectionately, as The Northern Git. It was a name he had earned when falling from the roof of a sort of medieval bus stop in the market square of the Dorset town of Beaminster, some twenty years previous, while still a student. The cracked bones that resulted ruled him out of selection for a game, hence the nick-name, bestowed by Crazey, our frustrated leader. Sam had something of a habit of falling off roofs. On a tour subsequent to the bus stop incident, after a game against the Dorset Rangers in the village of North Perrot in Somerset, he managed to fall two stories from the chimney of the pub to the pavement beneath the landlord's bedroom window. Fortunately he was not hurt, but, inconveniently, I remained perched on the thatched roof reassembling the village sign on top of the pub's chimney on my own. The landlord, woken by the whooshing and burbling noises escaping from the Northern Git as he landed heavily, and inane laughter coming through his ceiling, was not to be placated. Lancashire vowels coupled with my soft-southern silver spoon, low on hard consonants, seemed to deepen the landlord's displeasure. The result was the arrival of a police van containing two enormous policemen.

The Northern Git and myself, grinning idiotically and apologising for all we were worth, were duly handcuffed and removed from the scene of the debacle. Our arrest was short lived, for we were turfed out of the van in the middle of a misty moor, miles from the nearest town, one o'clock in the morning, with the gruff comments from the constables that "at least you are not in our patch any longer" and "make sure you beat them Devon lot tomorrow" (which was actually today, so to speak). They then drove off, leaving their ex-prisoners in the middle of nowhere. Quite sober by now, we thumbed a lift with an Exeter social worker driving a vintage Morris 1100, (what he was doing on the moor we never discovered), who very kindly went twenty miles out of his way to drive us back to our fellow cricketers in Dorset. We believe this to be the only incident of arrest in the seventy-odd-year history of the Rustic cricket tours, and remain very grateful to the merciful Exeter Samaritan for rescuing us from our foggy exile. This shared adventure created a lasting bond of friendship with Sam, so we were well received late at night at his Yorkshire home.

I woke very early on the monday morning. It was pitch black everywhere and I dared not turn the lights on for fear of waking our hosts. Eventually I located John, who liked his sleep and was not prone to my fits of over-excitement. He was pretty grumpy about being woken at three forty five in the morning. Explaining that we had 320 miles of our journey left, an optimistic estimate if he was navigating, that we had a storm to get through, a river to inspect and a shortage of daylight, I finally urged him into the car for a four o'clock departure. Three hours later we found ourselves travelling at a snail's pace on the A66 across the Pennines in torrential rain and winds gusting to 70 miles per hour. We passed a blown-over lorry, after which we pulled up at a little café to lash the canoe even more securely to the roof. As we drove away from the café (The Delli Llama where we had had an excellent breakfast), the third ratchet strap, which should have been firmly attached to the roof rack, slid loosely down the windscreen and on to the bonnet.

"John, I thought you knew how those straps worked." I said to him rather huffily.

"I do." He replied simply, giving me a rather pitying look. I knew his opinion of my mechanical skills only too well, so decided not to pursue the incompetence of his canoe-attaching any further. He appeared to be in a not-listening mood, a benign state of torpor that was a sort of mental equivalent to his ability to become lost physically. This condition was probably the explanation for the detached strap, I suggested. However, it was also true that I did find their workings very confusing.

The storm we were driving through had emptied the motorways, but our progress remained slow. The canoe acted like a sail, causing us to be blown all over the road. As we reached the great estuary of the Solway we saw large skeins of pink footed and barnacle geese being blown east at jet-speed in the hurricane gusts. By Glasgow, however, we had travelled out through the top of the storm cell in to more agreeable weather. The multitude of streams and rivers over which we drove were all swollen torrents coloured deeply with large amounts of silt. If the Dee were in similar condition, we would not be paddling. Our long journey could come to nothing. We passed the Earn, a tributary of the Tay. Even this pretty little river looked rather murderous in spate. The mighty Tay itself looked more foreboding still. I mentioned to John that the newly reintroduced beavers in the catchment would be facing extensive repair work to any dams they might have built during the gentler summer conditions. We started to discuss what adventure we might undertake as our canoe trip was beginning to look highly unlikely due to the dangers of such flood conditions.

"Shouldn't we have turned off to Braemar at Perth?" I asked John, rhetorically, as he had overruled the sat-nav by choosing to ignore its guidance altogether. He had a curious love of chaos, despite, or perhaps because of, having the mind of a scientist. (My 320 mile estimate would now be wrong by at least another twenty five.) We headed up the A9, following the swollen Tay to Pitlochry, where I made the unilateral decision to head east. This road climbed away from the valley of the Tay, and up into the tops of the Cairngorm mountains, through the bare but sun-lit slopes of Glenshee to where it ran parallel to the Clunie river, which accompanied us jauntily towards our destination. Red grouse abounded with many deer, but we did not see any golden eagles. The landscape of the Highlands breathed drama and wilderness in every direction. Even John began to look less sleepy and more interested. We had now arrived in the catchment of our chosen river. Our excitement grew, and we reached Braemar at about one o'clock.

I untied the canoe while John booked us in to our hotel, situated in the heart of the little town right beside the Clunie, and less than a mile from the Dee. We generally elected to stay in the hostelries closest to our rivers, and this one was perfectly located for a convenient entry to the water the following morning. Placing the canoe in front of the building, I then went to look for John, who was milling around in the hotel lobby. There then followed a highly embarrassing senior moment.

"Have you seen my reading glasses?" I asked him, absent-mindedly.

"Aaaah. They're on your head you fool!" He retorted. "Aaaah" was one of his favourite phrases, reserved mostly for moments of pleasure. His relish at my error was considerable, he even linked it to the earlier mess-up with the ratchet strap. I decided to go into the mountaineering shop, to escape him, where I bought a book on whitewater canoeing and engaged a young lady in conversation about our intention to paddle down the Dee.

"It'll be too high to do that today." She said, eyeing me carefully to assess whether I had completely lost my marbles. "We've had a lot of rain." Feeling a little discouraged by her obviously sensible observation, I then wandered out again collecting, by coincidence, the ambling John who was still smirking at my "lost" glasses.

We drove down the road to get our first view of the river Dee, curling through the unaffected Caledonian pine forest past the gentle fortification of Braemar castle. Though the light was leaving the day, the leaves on the trees were still holding their autumn colour, oak, birch and beech fringing the evergreen of the scots pines with tawny gold, reds and yellows. Kings and Queens had for generations fallen in love with this place, and its effect on two humble farmers was of equal power. The spell of this wonderful, wild glen was irresistible.

This first view of the Dee was misleading, as it was a fairly flat stretch. The beaches of gravel were covered by the risen water, which was moving quickly, but invitingly. It was not until we came to the first road bridge that we really saw the power of the beast. It surged through some large boulders and then dropped over three successive rock ledges in a sliding jumble of exploding water. It was frightening to look at, even from the safety of the bank. We muttered loudly, above the roaring sound, about "definitely portageing this bit." The light continued to fade as we descended the course of the river by the road which snaked along mostly near enough to see what we wanted. The Dee was mainly white, with long sections of the river marked by violently frothy short chop. Storm water levels smashed into boulder fields.

"It looks doable, if border-line, but not much fun," I muttered to John, not remotely believing the nervous utterance. The river did not look doable in the slightest. I felt scared at the prospect of getting into the canoe in this sort of maelstrom.

"Hmmm," replied John. "Definitely more difficult than I was expecting." He was seldom phased by any challenge, but I knew him well enough to note fear. "Hmmm" was the much used yang to his yin of "aaah". We carried on, inspecting one last rapid above the bridge at Dinnet, where we would be staying at the end of our first day of paddling. It had rolling waves, slanting across the river which I vigorously pronounced impossible in our open boat. We looked upstream, to a track sloping up from the river edge to the road. It provided a convenient get-out to carry the canoe past this brutal obstacle.

We found our second night's hotel a hundred yards or so from the bank, and, parking our Land Rover, caught the bus nearly twenty five miles back to the hotel at Braemar, where we had left the canoe. This seemed a tacit acknowledgement that we were actually going to canoe the following day, despite what we had seen. Neither of us said much on the journey, although I phoned home to tell Gundrada how beautiful the valley was, how dramatic the car journey had been and not to worry, even though the Dee was not quite as empty as it might be normally. I finished my call with the manly assurance to her that "we wouldn't do anything stupid." Later, I mentioned Boothie's words about dying to John who simply frowned and said how "sensible" the Scotsmen had been. We were both relieved that none of the other farmers were coming.

As usual we had researched a special subject to relate at one or other of our evening meals. We were in Royal Deeside so I had chosen to talk about the king of animals, the lion. During supper I held forth on the subject, and, for once, John took an interest. Neither of us really wanted to talk about the river, so lions occupied us for much of the evening. I had read an up to date account of lion conservation written by Craig Packer, the American professor in charge of the Serengeti research once championed by such great biologists as George Schaller and Bernard Grzimek. Lions face an extremely uncertain future, and the population left in the wild has dwindled to less than 20000. Conserving animals that eat children and cattle is extremely problematic. Dealing with corrupt politicians seemed equally so.

Man-eating lions featured in the presentation, in particular the legendary man-eaters of Tsavo. In 1898, during the building of the Kenya to Uganda railway, it was claimed by Colonel John Henry Patterson that two lions ate 135 of his native workers in a period of about six months. The story, though, was full of anomalies. One of the lions had a bad tooth, which some zoologists have claimed may have driven the animal to effect the dreadful massacre. Patterson, though, in his book, claimed to have knocked the tooth out with his rifle butt when charged while on guard one night, months after the killings had started. The Ugandan railway company claimed "only" 28 men were killed, though hundreds died from malaria and other illnesses brought on by poor working conditions.

The controversy has been recently re-examined by Justin Yeake at the Chicago museum of natural history, where the bodies of the two lions, who had eventually been shot by Patterson, were stored. Using samples of bone collagen and hair keratin, Yeake proved that they had indeed dined on humans, one lion eating the equivalent of eleven and the other twenty four poor souls.

John ruminated on this information, asking whether the lions had eaten already-dead humans, whose bodies most likely would have been thrown into the nearby Tsavo river, or indeed had only eaten the choicest pieces of live ones whom they caught, which would infer a higher total number killed to cause the hair and bone evidence. He asked, if the lions only ate say one leg per body, what the equivalent was in lives lost. John enjoyed pointless mathematical rumination of this sort but as Google was banned on canoe trips, we could garner no more relevant information. It was agreed that Yeake's work had served only to reawaken one of the horror stories of the African bush.

John then delivered his special subject, as usual involving complex theoretical physics, on the source of colour, but, tired after a very long day, I was out to spoil the lecture. I did not think highly of his largely incomprehensible presentation, not finding the colour orange that interesting at the best of times.

"Then why is granite pink?" I asked, knowing this would lead to childish admonishments and sniggering. The end of our evening thus arrived. Through the windows, as we retired to our respective beds, we could see rain running down the glass. Neither of us mentioned the Dee.

On the Tuesday morning I woke first, in the pitch black of pre-dawn. I finally got some life from John, and, without having looked at our river, we donned our canoe gear. John squeezed on a ramshackle collection of neoprene garments in addition to his wet suit. I climbed into my brand new dry suit, recently purchased at my local canoe shop after the stern advice of one of the instructors who worked there. It had many rubbery gaskets to stop water getting in anywhere, but was difficult to put on. While trying it on for size at the shop I had been ushered to a very small changing room, which, because I am over six foot four inches tall, was not apt for my physique. I became hopelessly tangled in the suit, getting wedged awkwardly in the tiny booth. As I debated whether to completely lose my dignity by calling for help, matters got worse when I heard my phone ring. I was supposed to be working. In a contortion of which Houdini would have been proud I answered, stuck and tangled though I was, and had a most business-like conversation with the conservation adviser from Natural England, with whom we were negotiating new nature conservation management agreements for our farm. I hoped Cath, the adviser, would never discover what was going on during that exchange.

After a brisk breakfast we collected the canoe and carried it to the edge of the tumbling Clunie river. We had our first view of what we were to face in the day ahead, chickened out and hefted the boat to a straighter section of the bank downstream. That was possibly the last sensible thing that we did over the next eight hours.

As always, leaving the bank was a moment of great release. We joined with the medium of the river embracing its pace and focussing completely on its ways. All our frets and worries melted to nothing, our spirits scampering delightedly at joining the current. The first obstacle on the river, after some fast bends, was a suspended stock fence spanning the whole width of the Clunie, just yards from where it united with the Dee. John and I had never encountered one of these before, and cautiously negotiated our way through the wooden slats while being bundled around by the swift chop. Catching the swirling waters, we then came onto the river we had travelled so far to enjoy. A gust of wind blew chill from the mountains, directly at our backs; we were in the cup of the old Irish blessing, "May the wind be always at your back."

I mentioned this to John, taking the credit for the organisation of such meteorological essentials and reminding him of the "winds of Berck" that we had encountered on a recent visit to France, which he had organised, or at least of which he had been nominally in charge.

"How far to the bridge?" he retorted, anticipating that there he would enjoy the undoing of my smug self-satisfaction, gained through the comparison with his organisation on the Autie.

The next mile or so was the only comfortable part of the journey. Hazy sunshine lit up the autumn colours, and the untrammelled ancient pine forest with its heather sprung floor and gnarled trees gave the setting deep serenity. I felt comfortable with yesterday's decision to portage the first set of rapids, so took the mood of our setting inwards. Relaxed completely, the ascending roar of the first rapid rudely interrupted.

I was steering, at the back, a position akin to being captain of the ship. Wholly at ease, I did not really appreciate the speed of the river, which had accelerated smoothly towards the churning drop. Very briskly we went beyond where we had thought we would get out at yesterday's cautious inspection. The time for portageing passed. We headed straight into the rough bouncing spray of the rock strewn narrow. As mentioned, the rapid here was a two-parter, luckily, and we made it really rather proficiently through vigorous surging water to a large eddy, half way down the morass. Snapping out of our somnambulist condition, we turned to the bank in the safety of the pocket of calm, and jumped out. We could add this to quite a long list of rapids descended that we had previously decided to avoid, though many had not such a successful outcome.

Re-entering the river below the successive rock shelves over which the water poured torrentially, our canoe bounced along on a boiling boulder field. The river was high enough to cover the majority of the smoothed granite stones, though sufficient remained prominent to warrant extreme vigilance and constant avoidance manoeuvers. John had taken over steering, so I was spotter, yelling out either "left" or "right" as we cascaded down river. His response was to ignore the advice entirely, and, as he could see the largest of the rocks, his method seemed to work. We remained at one with our little craft, if not with each other.

On rocks emergent, fresh with the peaty-white river spray, dippers abounded. The little birds stood proudly on jagged pinnacles sticking out everywhere in the swirling water. I had never seen a river so well populated by them. White fronted, the size of a robin with a chest like a little sergeant-major, they scavenge the rock edges and the river bed, using their tails to deflect the current and hold them under the surface, where they search for insects and crustacea. A Professor Krebs once suggested a theoretical experiment to quantify soil biota, involving a starling caged on a square metre of ground. The time it took the starling to starve to death was the measure, with the best soil being that which sustained the bird the longest. This was really a means by which he liked to emphasise the importance of the earthworm and its community of other soil dwellers. I felt that were he trying to quantify the health of the river, then he could use the dipper. However, I was quite happy to take numbers of dipper per mile of bank as sufficient measure of biological vigour, and not the length of life when caged per square metre..

I had to keep my thoughts entirely to myself, as there was only time simply to utter "dipper" between yells of "left," "right," and "would you bloody well steer, Dinnis." The Dee on this stretch passes down a narrow steep sided rocky valley, and under the first of two graceful white suspension bridges put there by Queen Victoria. Most of the day's journey took us through the Balmoral Estate, the Highland home of the Queen, and it is easy to see why she and her family are so happy on their visits here. However, with the river running so high and powerfully, I could not imagine any one fishing in any of its pools. Fortunate too, for a canoe interrupting the Duke of Edinburgh in mid cast over a salmon would probably have led to our execution. (Being November, the season was closed anyway). We had not seen a single person since leaving Braemar seven or eight miles up-stream. We had this pure-wild Eden to ourselves, gold leafed and split with this skipping water serpent. John suggested leaving the boat and visiting the Royal Estate, but we hadn't enough time. As a student he had worked on the Sandringham Estate in Norfolk, so claimed a slight history of royal association.

The Dee had yet more interesting characteristics to reveal. Normally, when on a canoe, one can see along the water to the horizon in front. Here we could see, sometimes, only thirty or forty metres ahead, then nothing as the river sloped away below our line-of-sight. It was unnerving not knowing what lay ahead, but so steep was the river's descent that we simply chose to trust our senses and read the water immediately upon us. We paddled on in a state of adrenalin-rich high alert.

Not long after passing the entrance to Balmoral Castle the river divided to go round a wooded island. We could see this clearly, and while looking ahead we neglected our present predicament. I was steering, and we hit a particularly rough section of whitewater that washed unhelpfully into the canoe. It filled the shell, sinking us. The water was cold and very powerful, and swept us down towards the island. Clinging on to the ropes we worked urgently to rescue the swamped boat. Ahead, the river divided into two narrow straits, each of which looked violently unmanageable, even if we had actually been in our boat. Buoyancy was no problem in my new dry suit and life jacket, and John, a human seal anyway, seemed not to be in too much difficulty either. Eventually we landed the canoe on the bank just before the river divided to bash its way round the island. We were relieved by our escape.

The jubilation prompted over-confidence, and we took to the water again to tackle the surge round the island. At one stage we managed to spin 360 degrees, a stunt that may have looked clever but which was accidental and rather scary given the rivers redoubled energy. My main recollection of this was scowling at John and he claiming to have had nothing to do with it. He had assumed, as I was steering at the back, that I had done it deliberately.

More boulder fields and whitewater ensued, the river providing constant challenge. There was no respite as the river rushed us onwards.

We reached the town of Ballater, at about one thirty, having had no prior opportunity for any food or drink. We ate a quick lasagne in a pub, sitting at a table with John dripping horribly while I had no such issue with my smart new dry-suit. Opposite was a man paralysed from the waist down and in a wheel chair taking his elderly mother out to lunch. He treated her with careful good manners and, on leaving, collected her coat, helped her on with it and then got to the pub door, before either John or I could move, and opened it for their exit. It was a sweet moment of gentleness, a counterpoint to the rigour of our voyage, but may also have signalled how exhausted we were.

After lunch we had to hurry to avoid darkness. Dinnet was still another six miles on, but this part of the river was a more even stretch, and the water had dropped noticeably since the morning. Pebble beaches were just visible and an ever greater number of rocks were strewn across our path. It seems that we had been lucky not just with the weather and the year's persistence with autumn colours, but with the exact water level we had enjoyed. Any lower and the river would have been a rocky misery, any higher and its obstacles would have been too dangerous. If I were to meet the girl in the Braemar shop again I would tell her that despite the strength of flow, the water had been perfect for our purpose. The voyage had been awesome, but was not over yet, despite the reflective mood bought on by lunch.

The shadow of night began its feline stalk. The already peaty water became an infinitely clear black. An elemental fear of the dark crept up on us as we paddled. I thought to myself about the geology we were experiencing, not just the granite, but an image that I had of obsidian, an extraordinary rock that comes from the same type of volcano as granite, but which is like black polished glass. At its most pure it is a gemstone. On Easter Island, far away in the Pacific, obsidian was used for the eyes of the great statues. The blackness of the water under us had the same infinite-seeming depth of oily colour. The water and the rocks around us were fast becoming a symphony of this cosmic shade. The depth of darkness sunk through the water with a bestial presence. If John's lecture of the night before had included black, I might have found his treatise relevant. I passed this on to him, but was ignored, so once more asked him if he knew why granite was pink. We were both tiring. I felt gripped by a powerful hallucination of the water's transparent, sable night. John then said, with some sense of wonder, "Isn't the water an incredible inkiness?" I reply "I think you may be going deaf." The blackness of the water was mesmeric. We carried on paddling in the spooky, surreal entrancement of the highland gloaming.

In our exhaustion we predictably ignored our observations of the previous day: when we had stood on the bridge at Dinnet we had gasped in horror at the rapid just upstream, and had made a sensible plan to haul out beforehand. It would have been a very sensible thing to do. Instead, falsely comforted by the slight drop in river level since we had last seen it, we silently agreed to have a go.

I was steering and managed an excellent line through the first section; I was even briefly optimistic of getting all the way down. Suddenly we had nowhere to go and quite literally nosedived into some quite large, rolling waves, which is never a good idea in an open canoe. It then sank beneath us and turned upside down. Canoe and men all completed the rest of the rocky jumble, separated from each other, finally spewing out the bottom of the rapid as if from a giant washing machine. Our problems were not over: we had to rescue the boat and all our luggage in the dry bags, but the river here was more powerful than ever. The pair of us were simply swept along, clinging to the up turned canoe. I had both the ropes, so left the comparative safety of the floating hull, and struck out vigorously for the bank. The canoe would not be steered, and would not budge from its central position in the surging river, no matter how hard I yanked on the rope.

There is a moment in a disaster when the mind eventually takes over from the instincts. I slowly realised what was going on. The canoe was extremely heavy, but John was still hanging on to it, trying to swim to the opposite bank while also seeking the ropes, both of which I already had in my hands. John resembled a seal in the power of his swimming as well as his aforementioned buoyancy. Their combined weight and his propulsion meant I could not get the boat to the right bank, nor myself, without letting go of the ropes. I shouted at him to let go, which, considering he had not listened to anything I had said all day, he miraculously did. The rescue happened smoothly once we co-ordinated our work, but such had been the tumult and effort involved in achieving safety that I had not noticed why I was finding swimming so difficult. My super-suit had started to fill with water, which of course I could not empty, as the gaskets seemed to have become one-way valves. It was.

quite an effort to finally gain the safety of the river bank, where I lay upside down on a slope and pulled the rubber-sealed neck open to allow the Dee to escape my person and return to its darkening bed. John was especially unhelpful when he saw what was happening, squatting down to laugh.

The plan on the following day had been to canoe a further 25 miles, getting us somewhere near the outskirts of Aberdeen. On rising at the appointed time, and over a superb breakfast at which we were the only guests, our plans took a change of direction.

"I've never been to Balmoral," said John, for the umpteenth time. "So, I've booked a guided safari of the Estate. It starts at ten."

I was feeling warm and dry, in comfortable clothes. The weather was grey. All of our canoeing kit was still wet. The river level had dropped, and would be much less fun than the trip we had completed. John had effected a fait-accompli of which I wholeheartedly approved.

"Let's get going, then," I replied, surprised at the willingness with which I relinquished a precious day on a river.

Epilogue
Postscript on prodding the bear

According to John

"Three waitresses all wearing black earrings. Talking about zombies and Singapore slings." The lyrics to my telephone ring tone announced that it was one of my daughters. "No trouble in their faces no anxious voice. None of the crazy you get from too much choice."

"Are we going to the Hole's?"

"Yes."

"Whoopee!"

It was a short conversation that confirmed the plans for the weekend, with children, wives and rickety farmers all looking forward to each other's company at a cross-country horse event being held at Montague.

I was driving home from a meeting with Martin. We had been reviewing the book. It was the first time that we had met to talk about past trips rather than arranging new ones.

We often used the phrases "carpe diem," seize the day, or "fill each minute with 60 seconds worth of distance run." Should we now revel in the fun of past adventure, or keep making new challenges? We sometimes hand the future too easily to our children and our lives become centred on degreasing the pole for their benefit. We do also have a duty to not neglect ourselves. My evening with Martin had refreshed my appetite for the many rivers to run and the attendant rejoicing in nature. The Test, the Dee, The Tees, the Tay and the Tyne, The Dordogne and the Danube delta all rose in the imagination as we chomped our supper. Can rivers keep coming up trumps? Our own experience was that each was better than the last.

We had met half way between our homes at a pub called the "Neville Crest and Gun," near Tunbridge Wells. In the bar I had been hollered at loudly, "Dinnis, you fool," after I had walked right past Martin. I had subconsciously eyed him on my arrival, not quite recognising the figure. A greying man in a shabby sweater and grubby shorts, that would have looked scruffy on a tramp, hunched over a book. In my mind's eye I was seeking a tall, good-looking man mountain. The figure from which the holler emanated was a weathered version. How much longer would we be lugging canoes up and down slippery banks, swimming in sub-zero waters or threading our craft over security fences and down spiral staircases?

Our evening followed the familiar Smith and Jones pattern, with much giggling, especially when, to get him off the subject of Gilbert White, I offered Martin the explanation of the length of the British coastline being dependent on the length of the tape measure. His vacant expression at my definition of fractals led to his comment, "If I shot an arrow at a hare, it could not reach its target. Zeno's paradox merely demonstrates that maths can be nonsense." Reviewing our book seemed to be dropping down the agenda.

He handed me the other book he had been studying when I had entered the pub. In the flyleaf was a handwritten dedication, signed by the author, "One drip to another." The author was a man called Dave Manby, the youngest of the six kayakers that had paddled The Dudh Khosi all those years ago, and the book was about rivers and canoe expeditions to places like The Indus, The Bramaputra, The North Fork of The Payette River and many other great runs. Martin was only looking backwards to inform his plans for the future.

During the meal we discussed our own book only briefly. We hoped it would just make people laugh. We also hoped that we succeeded in conveying something of the magic of the rivers and the friendship they had borne along their waters. Martin, with his customary passion for obscurity, said he thought the central point was made by me when listening to Nick's lecture on the Robin's Eye.

"I thought about the miracle of life......my appetite for the trip down the river tomorrow well and truly whetted".

"That's the point, really," I had playfully replied, "like poking the old bear in the corner of the room."

Martin had looked vacant, again, waiting for information, but, at the same time, looked around the room for a bear in one of the corners. The pub, though, was full of ordinary people coming and going, enjoying a quiet evening and avoiding the eye of the proverbial creature. I watched his face, amused, as he looked for the bear, and then, when the penny dropped, as he grinned at the conjured image.

"Yeup. You've just got to keep on poking," he said, before suggesting sympathetically that I should go to the opticians to take an eye test.

Martin offered to pay for the meal as he thought he hadn't paid for anything on The Authie trip. I reminded him that he had given me a wadge of cash at the time. As the waitress, pretty and blonde with blue eyes, brought over the credit card machine, he placed his glasses on his nose, studied the machine, and directed a lively gaze at her. His left eyebrow was raised. I winced in anticipation of an incident, but he proceeded to address both of us. "You must hear this story," he said "about the misreading of a text message. You know, I didn't have my glasses and I got the message from our shearing gang wrong, moving thousands of sheep and organising five or six men from the village to help get ready for a five a.m. start, when the message actually said they weren't coming until the following day."

The story took some time to complete, but that was its gist.

She smiled, as if humouring some exotic uncle, possibly not really understanding the mass movement of sheep that was being graphically described, nor the rather pointed references to failing eye-sight. She patiently reprogrammed the credit card machine that had timed out. I remembered, as we were leaving, that I had left my shoes in Martin's car, where they had been for the six weeks since our return from The Authie, and reminded Martin that he had said he would do the repairs on the canoe.

I assured myself, on my drive home, that our evening had not been full of signs of age-related enfeeblement, but, simply, the frayed capabilities that we had always had.

I was excited that we had many rivers still to run. I knew it would be a long time before we asked the question:

What shall we do after canoeing?

According to Martin

I didn't notice John enter the pub until he had walked past me and into the main area of the bar. I had, however, sat somewhere prominent so that he could see me, though the fact I had changed out of my usual work clothes and into something a bit smarter for the Neville Crest and Gun, may have had something to do with my new found invisibility. I also wondered whether, maybe, his eyesight was fading. John seldom looked uncomfortable, but sometimes he looks a little lost, like a wandering Wildebeest that has roamed from its herd. I watched him, over the top of my reading glasses, and waited for him to complete a fidgety circle as he peered at the other guests, still looking for me. He completed his circle, and now the other guests were discreetly eyeing this large ungulate who had been eyeing them. I could see he was vulnerable, so I yelled at him rather loudly, compounding his moment of exposure.

Hearing my customary hail of "Dinnis, you fool," across the crowded room, he realised he had been caught out, and ambled over with a grin on his muzzle. The other guests looked relieved to see the strange, isolated creature move to one of its kind. "This is written by one of the guys that did The Dudh Khosi," I said, offering him the book I had been perusing. I had opened it at a photograph which showed a tiny kayak in giant waves in a rocky river in a mountain gorge. It was a dramatic picture.

"I think we are here to talk about **our** book," said John.

"But ours will be just like this one," I stated. "Wilderness, adventure, drama and fun."

John's brow furrowed, and he gave me a slightly withering look before mentioning that The Cuckmere couldn't be compared to The Indus. However, I had done a bit of homework. "You know that Gilbert White, the naturalist, seldom left his home parish of Selbourne in Hampshire, and described the South Downs as "Majestic Mountains." His pen-friend, Joseph Banks, was off with Captain Cook discovering continents, mountain ranges and thousands of new species. That did not dampen White's ardour for natural history, nor the depth and richness of his appreciation for the world immediately around him."

"Which, of course, cannot be measured, because it depends on the size of the tape measure," John had continued, having arrived at what should have been an Editorial Meeting armed with some silly theory on fractals and perception, and intent on not letting me do the side-tracking.

We had an excellent supper and our book was discussed only sketchily. During the meal a lady in a fur coat came into the eating area, and sat nearby. I really began to wonder about John's sight in earnest when he began to talk about a bear being in the room, though he covered his tracks by pretending that he was actually making some metaphorical allusion.

By the end of the evening we had plans for several more expeditions, there being many rivers we wanted to visit. I felt we had been well looked after during the meal, the pretty young waitress, brunette and green-eyed, having been very attentive and clearly enjoying the attention of the men she was serving. I told her and John an extremely amusing story which she found funny, and I am sure I detected the merest hint of flirtation in her eyes when it was time to leave.

John and I split the bill, as he had forgotten that I had paid nothing towards our accommodation on The Authie. Before we went our separate ways, I handed John a bag containing his shoes, which he had also forgotten when we parted after our most recent trip. He then enquired as to whether "his" new canoe, which had taken a bit of a battering on the river six weeks earlier, had been repaired.

"Why?" I asked.

"Because there is a hole in my canoe," he said.

"We'd better hurry up and make another one," I replied.

References

Chapter 1

Sussex   Rudyard Kipling

Chapter 3

Catch 22   Joseph Heller

Chapter 4

Tarka the Otter Henry Williamson   Copyright credit to the Henry Williamson Literary Estate, c/o Anne Williamson annewatwork@gmail.com

The Tiger William Blake

Chapter 5

The Naming of the Shrew   John Wright

Chapter 6

Cricket report of the Irish Leprechauns 2014   Dick Forrest

The Windhover   Gerald Manley Hopkins

Ulyses and Finnegans Wake   James Joyce

Chapter 7

A Short Walk in the Hindu Kush Eric Newby

Chapter 11

Three Men in a Boat Jerome K Jerome

Waterlog Roger Deakin and *The Houghton Fishing Club Chronicles*

Chapter 12

Sonnet to the River Otter Samuel Taylor Coleridge

Chapter 14

Many Rivers to Run Dave Manby

Acknowledgements

Many thanks for ideas and encouragement go to our wives, Gundrada and Julie, and our children, Florence, Poppy, George, Romney, Rosie, Issie and Hattie. Their Uncles and Aunts (especially Sophia, Jane and Emma) and many of their cousins have also been both supportive and helpful. With reading, bearing in mind we are two farmers, special thanks to Dr Will Miller, who also authored most of the chapter on the January trip on the Wye, Tony Hamilton, who read two drafts and whose enthusiasm was superb, and several other fives players, cricketers, farmers and family friends, who also made the effort.

Thank you especially to Michael Fischer (and fiance Fritha Ross) for the illustrations, and useful guidance to improve the text.

All characters in this book exist in real-life, we think highly of you all and thank you for tolerating your respective roles in the stories. Particularly, thank you to those who have accompanied us on the expeditions in the book; Will, George Hosford, Stephen Armstrong, Nick Chapple, Patrick Hole, Gavin and Simon. And Nigel, even though he was always "too busy".

Thank you also to Paul Cooper and Paddy Butler for suggesting everyone has a book inside them, and that that is usually the best place for it!